The Melanin Effect 2

A Nutritional Path Back To Eden

Joseph "Jo Dash" Musa

authorHOUSE®

AuthorHouse™ UK
1663 Liberty Drive
Bloomington, IN 47403 USA
www.authorhouse.co.uk
Phone: UK TFN: 0800 0148641 (Toll Free inside the UK)
        UK Local: (02) 0369 56322 (+44 20 3695 6322 from outside the UK)

Published by AuthorHouse 09/29/2023

ISBN: 979-8-8230-8504-5 (sc)
ISBN: 979-8-8230-8505-2 (e)

Library of Congress Control Number: 2023918810

Contents

Chapter 1

This book was written to explore the systematic manipulation of food and how we have been disconnected from the fundamental elements of physical and mental biology. When you industrialise food to meet the demands of a growing public, you often find that addiction will become the sublevel mechanism that births the toxic relationship between individuals and food. After the 1940s, the industrialisation of food accelerated very quickly as economic and political shifts impacted social norms and attitudes. An easy example would be the mass of women who had to begin working after the world wars, which saw the home kitchen outsourced to the growing trend of restaurants and packaged foods. This allowed more preservation of food, which meant that we approached the biochemistry of the food chain by adding more chemicals to the food and adapting how it was cultivated. Somewhere in the 80s, we started to see an increase in calories in meals, especially the dessert options in restaurants and fast-food chains. Food high in artificial sugars and trans fats and low in nutritional value became the frontier of mass food addiction and chronic health diseases.

Since health is truly the only real wealth on this planet, it's very clear that we have allowed ourselves to fall too far from the path. The very true essence of health revolves around our relationship with nature. This means the closer we are to our indigenous dietary makeup, the closer we are to our truest version of holistic health. In *The Melanin Effect Book 2: A Nutritional Path To*

Eden, we start unpacking this ever-growing strenuous and toxic relationship with food.

We will also look at what type of diet is best for humans and how mindful eating is the best practice to slow down the mass food-related diseases affecting humanity. Dr Sebi, Dr Llaila Afrika, Dr Arnold Ehret and Dr Catherine Shannan, to name a few, have devoted their lives to educating, informing and providing long-lasting solutions to handle our relationship with food. Like those before me, we have seen a future that threatens humankind's mortality and quality of life. If we are to see significant and effective changes in society and how we deal with food, we must be nutrition-conscious and find better, safer ways to cultivate and package food for the masses. The concept of an "Untitled Diet" can pose as an enigmatic proposition on how we should eat to live, not eat to die. Once we can learn to respect the internal status quo more than the things we externalise, food will once again take centre stage in the conversation of medicine and health.

A Brief History of Food

Food can be defined as nutritional content that allows the body to grow, metabolise, and sustain and repair cells. We can define something as food-based on the principle that it can give you energy and promote health. The word "food" has interesting Proto-Indo-European roots, where its ancestral meaning lies in the ancient Greek word *pateisthai*, meaning "to feed". When discussing the word "feeding", we have to understand it's about "nourishment", which means supplying an organism with the nutrients required to build and sustain health.

For over 200,000 years, humans have been hunting, gathering, building and constructing their lives around the availability of food. Food is the essential element that determines whether or not a civilisation can settle somewhere and if it is inhabitable, enough food can be found. It is no secret that food has been the centre of our biological universe and still holds that position today. As far as 11,000 BCE, independent pockets of the world such as the Middle East, China, Sub-Saharan Africa and Central America saw a gradual shift from hunter-gathering to cultivating crops and rearing animals for food. It is difficult to pinpoint the exact reason for the shift from hunter-gathering to the agricultural approach. However, we can safely assume key factors such as climate, overhunting, population growth, and the use of domesticated seeds may have laid the foundation for such change. We will dive into each of these key factors so we can really look at how each gave rise to agriculture as we know it.

Climate Factors

A team of climatologists and anthropologists found that places in Africa, such as the Northeast, were known to be warm and wet about 130,000 to 80,000 years ago. However, somewhere between 75,000 and 55,000 years ago, the climate turned dry and cold, making hunting and gathering more difficult and at times impossible. It is said that the migration of humans out of Africa may have been out of necessity as climates changed to search for fertile environments to gain access to food.

Greater Population Density

As the population grew among tribes, the demand for more food from the wild grew beyond the ability and resources to hunt. Each tribe at that point had already developed divine systems based on spirituality, customs and astrological shifts to hunt and gather food. And as the tribe grew, so did the need to adapt and create sustainable means to meet the demands of everybody. Farming provided adequate food per acre despite the fact that it required more time and energy to cultivate.

Overhunting

Overhunting has been the cause of the serious reduction of certain species, including the extinction of animals, insects, sea creatures, etc. Hunting and gathering were a stable part of how communities obtained food 200,000 years ago. After hunting food for a few thousand years, it would be inevitable to see the decline in species that were a centre point of their diet. According to paleoanthropologists, clothing from animals that would have otherwise provided warmth over the winter would have been a foreseen problem.

Domesticated Seeds

Domesticated seeds are variants selected by humans, varying their genetics over time and causing morphological changes that allow crops to differ from their wild relatives. Domesticated crops have been transformed, sometimes beyond recognition from their indigenous relative, based on man-made environmental manipulations to support the mass cultivation of crops.

History of Cooking with Fire

The genesis of cooking has been a difficult event to pinpoint, but it is the belief of some culinary and palaeoanthropology scholars that early man might have first stumbled across burnt meat from wildfires. Upon savouring such meat, early man might have found that heated meat was more palatable, but there is insufficient evidence to really support this theory. In fact, other scholars agree that evidence of burnt ashes and animal bones from the Wonderwerk Cave in South Africa 1.8 million years ago suggests the use of controlled fire was already in effect. This may have been the sole cooking technique until the Palaeolithic period, also known as the Old Stone Age. We see the emergence of more advanced tools much further down the line by early

Africans using cooking in a systematic measure derived from the practice of using heat in alchemy. One may struggle to get a more accurate picture, given that the evidence is scattered. Therefore, we can only assume that cooking may have started medicinally before becoming part of dietary practices. However, most of Africa was feasting on fruits, grains and vegetables. The concept of eating meat came much further down the line – about 1,800 BCE.

Cooking in Medieval Europe in the 5th to 15th Centuries

The Middle Ages, often referred to as the Dark Ages or mediaeval times, was a very expensive time for food, and only the rich ate very well. It is called the Dark Ages specifically because of the suppression of cultural, scientific and technological advancement. Europe was overrun with famine and disease, which meant that the food quantity was low, and the poor ate very basic food, including oats, rye, barley, peas and broths. Since food was also a symbol of status, it was expensive. The rich ate various types of meat, some of which modern diets would not even consider food.

The nutritional content of mediaeval Europe was filled with high levels of carbohydrates from oats and barley (beer), alongside vegetables and a moderate number of fruits. However, this varied from region to region, depending on availability and class. Protein from meat was eaten sparingly amongst those of lower social status.

Nothing went to waste in mediaeval Europe, and without refrigerators, freezers or other effective means of preservation, it was necessary to consume – or at least make the best of – what you had.

Grains

A food product that was common amongst all classes was cereal, which made up the majority of the population's caloric intake. People of aristocratic status would very often prefer cooking wheat, as it was expensive to acquire and could be used to make bread or porridge. Besides the upper class, the majority of the working lower class of Europe did not consume a lot of bread for similar yet opposing economic reasons. This meant that with lower macronutrient-to-macronutrient ratios, most of Europe would not have had great immune systems, which meant disease would be easy to catch.

Fruits & Vegetables

Vegetables made up the largest portion of the mediaeval nutrition food group. Onions, garlic, carrots, legumes, chickpeas and fava beans would be used to make stew and other dishes across different regions. Agriculture in colder climates made food seasonal, with only the rich having access to a constant flow of fresh produce throughout the year. Fruits like strawberries, grapes and apples were often used as starters to be eaten before a main meal. Now, if you lived in a region where oils, such as olive oil, were procured, they were primarily used to cook.

Protein

Fish was a key source of protein amongst all classes, even though the upper class and royals would have far more options for food. External factors like religious influence regulated the amount of food consumption, such as Fridays being a fast day imposed by the Catholic Church. Groups of people who lived on the coastline had ready access in comparison to their inland neighbours. Furthermore, preservation techniques like smoking and salting allowed practical exportation so everyone could have access to fish, people had access to proteins and healthy fats.

Nutritional Status in Medieval Europe

People were often under the impression that eating food with specific properties in a certain order would result in proper digestion. The thinking behind this is that the lighter, lower-calorie foods should be consumed first and the heavier main meals last. It was assumed that the heavier foods would sink to the bottom of the stomach and affect proper digestion in such a way it would give the food enough time to rot in their intestines. Another interesting thing worth mentioning is food was often looked at from scales of warm-to-cold and moist-to-dry based on ancient Greek medicine culture. So, the preparation of food and its temperature were factors to be considered in proper digestion, with a preference towards warm and moist foods.

Nutritional Summary of Medieval Europe

There are many factors to consider when looking at the overall nutritional status of the Middle Ages, such as socioeconomic changes, variations in climate, and which crops were accessible from region to region. What we do know is all classes had a high carbohydrate intake from foods such as cereal, porridge and a lot of beer. Fish and meat were consumed in moderation amongst the lower class and readily consumed by the upper classes. The impact of a modest diet and mostly highly physical lifestyle amongst the lower class left people in a caloric deficit, and only the rich and their lavish lifestyles were able to be overweight due to overconsumption.

The lower-class macronutrient intake ratio was likely around **60–75% carbohydrates**, **15–25% protein** and **10–20% fats**, with very little caloric overconsumption. The macronutrient consumption ratio among the upper class and religious clergy is estimated to have been around **55–65% carbohydrates**, **20–30% protein** and **15–25% fats**, with a high chance of caloric overconsumption.

African Food Culture

Over time, ingredients and cooking techniques have evolved historically across Africa. Before the dawn of intercontinental trade with other neighbouring natives, some of the most common cultural foods included millet, fonio, barley, lentils and, on rare occasions, rice. In the East African region of the continent, we see an Arab, Persian and Indian culinary influence on cosmopolitan food culture and local diets. The impact on the local diet was due to the importation of sugarcane, spices, dried fruits and rice, which greatly influenced the region's palate. As time passed (a lot of time), broader influences on the local diet came from places like China and India. Here, we see the importation of fruits such as bananas, oranges, lemons and some domesticated animals such as pigs.

500 BCE Dining in Africa

Grains were initially domesticated from the wild grass of the savannah west of the Egyptian Nile, and sorghum (cereal) has been one of the most significant foods in the African continent. Other indigenous African savanna grasses, like millet, were also a staple food of high dietary importance on the African continent. Different types of millet, such as pearl millet, originated from the western Sahel and started to make its way throughout the rest of the African continent. Other types of millet, such as finger millet, are native to Ethiopia, and other Eastern African Highlands tend to stay in those regions. The Bantu people, who are a collection of tribes from the sub-Sahara that speak many languages, allowed the migration of yams throughout other parts of the continent. However, during the transatlantic trade, yams were taken over to the Caribbean and later became a key part of Caribbean, Southeast Asian and Oceanic diets. Other indigenous foods like guinea rice originated in the hot, wet Guinea Coast. The delta basin in the Niger River spread to other parts of Africa and influenced the West African diet. A thousand years ago, food from Southeast Asia made its way to the East African shores by traders using the trade winds. This was after the Arabs had taken control of the maritime trade routes from the east of Africa to the Indian shores. The Swahili tribe, whose native food name is "finger millet mjengo", meaning "construction worker food", had this superfood that provided high energy and fibre to their diets. These cereals were accompanied by other edible vegetation. However, as trade influenced the nutrition of the country, changing the people's daily intake, hidden hunger was prevalent due to not enough vegetation being eaten. Hidden hunger is caused by micronutrient deficiencies, especially with vitamin A, iron and iodine. An interesting fact also worth mentioning is that the Bantu people, for the most part, ate sweet potatoes, bananas, plantains, millet, wild vegetables, wild berries, etc. The cooking method was not elaborate, and food satisfaction took precedence over enjoyment as the chief purpose of eating at these times.

There Are 3 Ways Africans Develop Strong

Nutritional Spirituality:

1. **Practising Meditation**: Meditation is a practice best suited to help increase a person's self-awareness. Having the right food groups that balance mood and promote focus are a key part of the dietary lifestyle (omega-3, magnesium L-threonate and vitamin B3).

2. **Fasting:** Abstaining from food lets the body develop emotional, mental and spiritual balance. Certain food groups

tend to destabilise a person's vibration. However, fasting can cleanse the body and clean the blood so you may heighten your spiritual power.

3. **Conscious Eating**: Mindful eating means prioritising nutritionally rich food to nourish the body instead of impulsive feeding on high sugars and unhealthy fats.

Indigenous Cultures & Nutrition

Indigenous cultures have always recognised the dual role food plays in the spiritual and physical aspects of their society. For example, the Native Americans only ate meat that was believed to be sacred, Hinduism forbids eating meat and Sub-Saharan tribes focused on foods provided by nature. Conversely, there are foods believed to be spiritual or bestow spiritual powers, and ceremonial occasions require stricter food selection to help strengthen spiritual connections. In places such as Peru, shamans perform "Icaro", a healing song often administered alongside a medicine man's purification diet. The diet requires individuals to refrain from salt, sugar or meats. They are given spiritual foods such as ayahuasca and other indigenous herbs to induce a profound state of healing, awareness and balance. When it comes to holistic health, it comes down to having a high degree of mindfulness on what we take in and leave out to achieve a constant state of biological and spiritual balance. This is important at times when there are many conflicting choices when it comes to food, what we eat, what's good and what's not. Our innermost, deepest truth speaks through the consciousness to remind us how we truly feel about our health. Only when we are able to still ourselves and listen to that intuitive self can we truly know what is good for our minds, bodies and souls. The nutritional messages received from our bodies are transmitted in many different ways, from genuine hunger, cravings, disease, addiction, allergies, physical discomfort and energy levels.

There are some key principles to understand when it comes to how nutrition has evolved and changed over the years. The first thing is to consider that all over the world, people were eating as part of a collective cultural lifestyle. This means that everybody ate what everyone else ate in their native surroundings and participated in the communal practice of preparing, harvesting and gathering food. Second, indigenous cultures around the world ate out of necessity and often via standard cultural practices. This means people dealt with food on a need-to-eat basis.

Chapter 2

Fasting

It is a popular assumption that "fasting" often involves an act of starvation. In fact, the word "fasting" is based upon a period of abstinence from food, whereas starving denotes a form of suffering, forcing or depriving one of food. The difference is significant, and thus, highlighting its distinction lets us know exactly what we are doing when we embark on a health journey such as fasting. Historically, human beings have always practised a form of fasting as an intricate part of human anthropological well-being. The word "fasting" has its root word in old English *fæsten*, which means fortress or enclosure. This speaks directly to the general understanding that abstaining from food protects the body so it may metabolise itself back into perfect homeostasis.

Different Types of Fasting

As fasting gains more traction and starts to permeate our social norms, we must get a clear picture of the different types of fasting and their implications. When fasting is not done properly, it can become dangerous and cause more problems than it solves.

- **Water Fasting:** Water fasting refers to abstaining from food and drink containing calories for an extended period of time. Often advised for up to 72 hours at a time, including a pre-examination by a physician to make sure you are in the best condition to practice such fasting. The key takeaway is that water fasting can be very effective holistically on the body, even sparking increased body performance and stem cell production.

- **Juice Fasting:** Juice fasting refers to drinking primarily fruits and vegetables as part of a cleansing and detoxification process. This type of fast is very popular, especially within the vegan community. It is part of alkalising to reduce oxidative stress in the body. Typically, a period of 1–10 days is recommended to experience the best results, and while great for weight loss, it will be temporary until you begin to consume solids again.

- **Intermittent Fasting:** Also referred to as intermittent energy restriction, intermittent fasting involves a calorie-restrictive diet within designated time periods throughout the day. This means an individual will create a feeding window, usually between noon and eight at night, where the individual will stop eating. This popular method is known as the 16:8 method, meaning 16 hours of fasting followed by an 8-hour window for food consumption.

- **Partial Fasting:** This refers to abstaining from processed food, animal products and high glycaemic drinks to provide a cleaner way of eating. Partial fasting can benefit anyone and can be implemented at any point. Removing harmful foods from your diet automatically improves your overall well-being. You can practice partial fasting for more extended periods or several days of the week and enjoy major benefits.

- **Dry Fasting:** Dry fasting, better known as "absolute fasting", is the mother of all fasting, where you abstain from food and water for a short period. There are huge benefits with this as far as neurogenesis, anti-inflammation, balanced insulin levels and cellular repair. However, if you are new to fasting, up to 24 hours would be a starting point, and the more experienced can go for weeks and, sometimes in rare moments, months. Limited water intake encourages your body to burn more fat. For every 100 grams of fat, your body produces 107–110 grams of water.

Conclusion

The reality about fasting is that when done properly and with the right guidance, it can be one of the best things you can do to push your body into self-regeneration. Fasting when pregnant or breastfeeding is not recommended, as well as those with certain physical or mental illnesses.

The Significant Role of Fasting in Religion

In ancient times, civilisations would practice fasting as part of a religious commitment. This would especially apply to priests or priestesses initiating or preparing to connect with their respective deities. In the ancient Greek Hellenistic religion, total dedication was rewarded by the deities with divine teachings and visions in the dreams of the devotee. In pre-Columbian parts of Latin America, the locals would fast for periods of time to seek repentance or mercy from an angered deity who would otherwise smite their crops and allow plagues to devour villages.

Some Native American tribes practice fasting on vision quests, either during or after, to complete the spiritual lesson. The indigenous Tungusic people of Northern Russia also participated in fasting in their shaman religion to help amplify spiritual connection and healing abilities. The priesthood of the Pueblo Native Americans of Southwestern America would often fast during spiritual retreats as part of a major ceremony relating to seasonal changes. In the Western religions of Christianity, Judaism and Islam, fasting is emphasised seasonally in veneration towards their chosen deity. Very specific dietary laws and practices were to be strictly observed in order to purify and cleanse the body in hopes of receiving spiritual connection and blessings. In Judaism, Yom Kippur is the holiest day of the year for atonement. Fasting is practised during Yom Kippur to slow down your biological rhythm to create a calmness that will allow profound inner spiritual revelations through self-reflection. In early Roman

Catholicism, 40-day fasting periods would be observed before Easter and during Advent, a period of atonement before Christmas. This fasting custom in early Catholicism has since been adjusted to allow significant individual choice during the 2nd Vatican Council between 1962 and 1965. However, protestant churches still require members to practice the fasting period of Lent. In Islam, fasting is one of the core pillars of the religion, which requires participants to abstain from material experiences and connect with the creator more personally. It is believed when Muslims journey through the fasting experience, their heart is awakened, and they embody total submission to the will of Allah, the Exalted. During the fasting period, the servant goes through self-purification, where the body's circadian rhythm is placed in harmonious balance. This is important because abstaining from food, drink, and other forms of earthly pleasure brings about an inner clarity that reveals God's word.

Biological Impacts of Fasting

There have been many myths surrounding the benefits of intermittent fasting, and some of its anecdotal claims may actually have their inception in science. Consequently, I will dive into the biological realms of fasting to show what is scientific truth versus fallacy. One of the key essential metabolic responses to fasting in the body is autophagy, where cells go through a clean-up and repair phase. Your cells want to grow and divide as part of a natural biological cycle of life. However, without efficient cellular waste removal via autophagy, your cells risk becoming cancerous and can evolve into harmful tumours. Later sections will dig a little deeper into the wonderful world of autophagy, but to begin, there are several benefits that have solid scientific grounds that are worth mentioning, including regulation of blood sugar and blood pressure, anti-inflammatory properties, weight loss, boosted brain function and anti-ageing benefits.

Blood sugar: Studies have shown that intermittent fasting can significantly regulate blood sugar levels, increase your resistance to stress and reduce inflammation. Fasting influences glycogenolysis, which is when a decreased caloric intake means less insulin is produced, so the body goes through a process of using stored glucose from your liver for energy. This is very beneficial for people with diabetes because 2–4 weeks of fasting can drastically improve blood sugar. Blood sugar levels typically are at their highest in the morning from about 3 to 8 a.m. to help prepare the body with enough energy for the day. Fasting pushes the body to regulate blood sugar by creating homeostasis within the blood, pulling excess sugar out of the blood and into the muscles and other organs for energy.

Blood pressure: One of the amazing benefits of fasting is an increase in what is known as parasympathetic activity. This is very important because parasympathetic activity regulates blood pressure under resting state. If too much blood is pushed through the artery at a time, your heart has to work harder, and this stress can lead to some form of heart failure or a potential stroke. The parasympathetic system controls any abnormal increase in blood pressure because it triggers what is known as the baroreceptors reflex. This causes blood vessels to relax, decreasing resistance to blood flow and decreasing your heart rate, regulating blood pressure back to normal. Lastly, avoiding processed foods high in sodium or bad fats during your eating window (if you are intermittently fasting) is key in keeping your blood pressure in the normal region.

Anti-Inflammatory properties: Inflammation is the body's autoimmune response to foreign invasion, calling upon your red and white blood cells as part of the inflammation process. In a fasting state, your body reduces the amount of monocyte pro-inflammation cells in the bloodstream. Studies show that the monocyte population of an area is dependent on glucose and protein levels in the blood. Since you are eating less, less glucose will be floating in your blood to trigger the autoimmune response for monocytes to populate.

Weight loss: Fasting restricts the body's calorie intake whilst continually using reserved energy to create a caloric deficit. Your basal metabolic rate is the exact amount of energy your body needs for basic bodily functions such as digestion, breathing, synthesising and transporting. All these biological activities take up a small percentage of calorie burn, while activities like exercise account for an additional 5–10% (hence why counting steps increases your chances of weight loss). During your fasting period, your body uses glucose initially before moving on to fat to burn for energy. However, understanding the vital role hormones play in this process is key – hormones such as insulin, ghrelin, adiponectin, leptin, etc. All of these hormones regulate hunger and satiety responses as well as fat storage. When fasting, you decrease ghrelin and increase leptin, making you less hungry.

Consequently, you're ingesting less food, which means less insulin to store excess glucose in the blood as fat.

Boost brain function: Intermittent fasting has been proven to induce the secretion of a growth factor known as Brain-Derived Neural Factors (BDNF). This very important protein is boosted during fasting by up to 400%.

Also known as "Miracle Grow for your brain", these neurotrophic factors cause the brain to adapt to external stimuli, making your mind more robust by boosting memory, mood and learning. The brain is primed to do this through the growth of new neurons via neurogenesis, which takes place in the hippocampus, where learning and memory are vital. The formation of neuronal connections is another way BDNF affects the brain, causing synaptogenesis, which is when brain cells link to form structures. This end-to-end synapsis connection boosts cell-to-cell communication. Another key aspect to mention is that BDNF deficiencies have been connected to various cognitive impairments or psychological conditions, such as dementia, Alzheimer's, schizophrenia and depression.

Anti-ageing benefits: Calorie restriction has been connected to some of the underlying ageing factors by slowing down the DNA mortality rate. As we age, DNA degradation is a normal part of life, and fasting seems to accelerate DNA repair. Consequently, the rate of DNA degradation will slow down and keep cells optimal for longer. On a larger scale, fasting will stimulate the increase of antioxidants in the body. This is a very important process because it prevents free radicals from breaking down cells, and free radicals are very harmful to cellular health. So, if you're looking to create an optimal environment in your body to keep you feeling 20 when you're over 50, fasting can be a very effective way to achieve that goal.

What Is Intermittent Fasting?

Intermittent fasting refers to a process of structured calorie restriction. This can be broken down into a 16-hour fasting period followed by an 8-hour window of healthy and nutritional eating. Different types of intermittent fasting work for all different sorts of scenarios. You can fast a warrior fast, which constitutes one meal a day, or you can do the 5:2 diet, where you restrict calories five days a week and return to an average calorie intake over the weekend. There are several other effective methods that consist of allowing calorie intake for designated hours and managing prolonged hours of fasting. Even though Martin Berkhan of Leangains.com is credited for popularising the term "intermittent fasting", the truth is calorie restriction is far more ancient in its conception. Humans have evolved their relationship with food to the point where it has become a liability instead of a healthy asset. Over 12,000 years ago, human beings only ate for one reason and one reason only: survival. With a deep connection and understanding of their circadian rhythm, humans ate according to the moon and sun's cycles. The whole point of food is to add fuel, helping the body grow and function harmoniously. However, as long as you use intermittent fasting symbiotically in your lifestyle, you will be able to enjoy many of the benefits that intermittent fasting has to offer.

Best Ways to Intermittent Fast

There are several ways to intermittent fast effectively. The key thing to remember is to exercise, eat nutritionally and stay hydrated. Having said that, there are some conditions that determine if intermittent fasting is suitable for an individual. These include breastfeeding or pregnant women, those grossly underweight or struggling with an eating disorder, those under 15 or over 75 years old, or those struggling with weight gain. In certain conditions, you might have to adjust fasting times around certain medications if they still permit you to fast. The first thing you should do when you want to start is plan the time frame you want to fast for, find the food that you need to aid your fast, and meal prep. This is important because it will allow you to know what you are going to be eating without the distraction of peripheral choices. Include an average of 2 litres of water because hydration is important to aid metabolism and help optimise your nutritional meals. Lastly, exercise will be very powerful, especially for weight loss and keeping the body optimal during the fasting periods. Finally, being able to do it in groups or with a friend proves far more effective, especially because of group support and accountability.

Biological Stages of Intermittent Fasting

Intermittent fasting will stimulate chemical reactions and other metabolic and anabolic processes to take place throughout the fasting hours. I have broken down the process into five simple stages for further insight.

Stage 1 (18–12 hours): Fasting technically starts around 8 hours after our last meal when blood sugar drops and stimulates your body for feeding. Around this point, it is normal to experience cravings, fatigue and hunger. It is extremely important to have a strong emotional grip on your hunger to survive this point. If you can persevere through this point till about 12 hours, you initiate mild ketosis, and your fat-burning mechanisms start to activate. This will deplete your glycogen storage, stabilising blood sugar levels and switching over to breaking down fat cells instead of carbohydrates.

Stage 2 (13–18 hours): By the 16–18-hour mark, your body will be in a state of ketosis, and stored fat will become your body's primary source of fuel. At this point, your ketogenesis is taking place in the liver to produce ketones that will be released back into the bloodstream. Essentially, these ketones nourish the brain, help reduce inflammation throughout the body and stabilise insulin levels. You will also experience improved mood, mental clarity, alertness and efficiency due to the production of BDNF in the brain.

Stage 3 (19–24 hours): Around the 19th hour, your body enters a cellular recycling phase known as autophagy. Autophagy is a clever way your body self-cleans and removes any damaged cellular materials or waste out of the cells. This key process keeps your cells optimal and functioning efficiently, keeping the body healthy. Excessive cellular waste build-up can lead to certain neurodegenerative diseases and carcinogenic cells developing in chronic conditions, such as Alzheimer's or dementia. Autophagy happens less frequently as we mature, so implementing a quick 24-hour fast weekly can take years off your biological age.

Stage 4 (36–48 hours): Human growth hormones (HGH), also known as somatropin, are essential to building tissue, repairing tissue, boosting metabolism, burning fat, encouraging cellular production and are instrumental in children's growth. As you fast, you reduce insulin levels in the blood, allowing the pituitary gland to produce more HGH. Low levels of HGH in the body have been linked to obesity, low sex drive, anxiety and much more. Fasting past the 48-hour mark increases HGH by 400%, which is great news for the body as HGH are key for the body to develop. When enough HGH are not produced in children, it is known as Growth Hormone Deficiency, which leads to a condition known as pituitary dwarfism.

Stage 5 (72+ hours): A complete overhaul of the immune system takes place in Stage 5 – immunity. After three days of fasting, you start to push cellular regeneration, and stem cells are produced to improve the body's twelve systems and push your immune system to optimal levels. This can be very powerful when you have the flu, improving your body's defence mechanisms to fight off infections or improving the effectiveness of some treatments.

The Science of Autophagy

The word autophagy can be broken down into "auto", meaning self, and "phagy", meaning eat or to devour. Essentially, autophagy is the process also known as autophagocytosis, whereby lysosomes, a membrane-bound organelle containing enzymes, break down cellular debris and other intracellular molecules that are worn out or cause cellular waste build-up. During autophagy, these lysosomes increase acidification to help break down these cells, and sometimes, these lysosomes are called upon to neutralise invading viruses and bacteria. The important thing is your body has to do this process as regularly as possible. As we age, our body tends to do this less. So integrating intermittent fasting or just regular water fasting at times can keep autophagy constant. Autophagy can be a very powerful tool known to work against viral infections after a study on yeast saw an increase in autophagy activity through prolonged nutritional starvation. The process of cellular degradation of damaged proteins or worn-down cells allows autophagy to be very effective in recycling these proteins and neutralising harmful cellular activity. So, if a cell has a virus, autophagy will regulate the inflammation response and start cellular degradation to potentially stop any spread of the virus. However, certain viruses, such as the herpes virus, have a gene that blocks autophagosome maturation to manipulate autophagy, which allows them to evade the immunity response whilst benefiting from the cellular environment autophagy provides. However, the autophagy process helps remove toxic proteins that can lead to neurodegenerative diseases and prevent the accumulation of cellular waste and other proteins linked to the main cause of the body's ageing.

Hormones & Fasting

Fasting modulates a plethora of biological systems in the body, and hormones are no different in this matter. Your hormones carry out a multitude of functions, from signalling, regulating, transporting and communicating with the biological systems regarding what to do and exactly when to do it. Essentially, your hormones coordinate day-to-day mental, emotional and physical responses to both external stimuli and internal movements. Fasting allows hormones to regulate themselves to stabilise blood glucose, inflammation response, fat storage capacity, blood pressure, cognitive functions and so much more. Let's look at specific hormones, how they respond to a fasting state and what type of benefits can be expected.

Serotonin: Serotonin, also referred to as 5-hydroxytryptamine (5-HT), is a neurotransmitter predominantly produced in the gut that is essential in nerve cell communication and is key in mood regulation, emotional responses, appetite, digestion and plays an intricate role in the circadian rhythm. Serotonin is also a precursor to melatonin synthesis pathways in the brain that regulate your sleep-wake cycle. Serotonin abnormalities can result in depression, anxiety, anger, agitation, suicidal thoughts, poor dieting options, and so much more. However, when we fast, we increase serotonin by improving 5-HT turnover all over the brain. This is great because this means signalling pathways are more efficient. As a result, we experience a boost in mood, hunger regulation, higher cognitive function and a strong sense of self.

Consequently, eating healthy, nutritious food during fasting could make this process far more effective and produce more satisfying results.

Melatonin: Melatonin, also known as *N*-acetyl-5-methoxytryptamine, is an essential hormone exclusively secreted by the pineal gland to regulate multiple body functions and regulate the sleep-wake cycle in synchronicity with serotonin. Melatonin also plays a vital biological role in the retina for light signalling, innate cellular immune response, insulin secretion by inhibiting beta-pancreatic cells, dilation, contraction of blood vessels and regulation of sexual hormone releases as melatonin receptors are expressed throughout the body. When we fast, we increase melatonin productivity, which is phenomenally effective and beneficial for the entire body. First, melatonin regulates insulin release, meaning HGH can increase at night, which is key for body growth and general well-being. Fasting also increases the quality of sleep, which affects mood, reduces stress, increases immunity, increases cognitive function and helps manage a healthy body weight.

Insulin: Insulin is an anabolic hormone produced in the pancreas by beta cells in order to regulate blood glucose and metabolise fats, proteins and carbohydrates in the body. Insulin is released every time you eat in order to carry out the essential process of breaking down the food's components for energy and storage. When we eat food with a high glycaemic index or food with tremendous amounts of processed fats, insulin spikes, and over a long period of time, insulin resistance can develop. Developing insulin resistance means your muscles and tissues no longer respond correctly to insulin and instead will pull directly from the bloodstream. When this happens, your pancreas makes a whole lot more insulin, which can cause severe problems, such as too much glucose in the blood, increased weight gain and potentially type 2 diabetes. Fasting allows your body to regulate insulin production because the calorie restriction allows the insulin levels to normalise and work far better.

Leptin: This hormone is known as the satiety hormone because it regulates feeding capacity. Produced in the small intestine by adipocytes (fat cells), it works hand in hand with other hunger hormones such as ghrelin, adiponectin and melanin. The essential purpose of leptin is energy balance and storage regulation. Depending on feeding times in your fast, sex and weight, leptin will adjust to regulate the energy balance where necessary. For example, leptin levels are higher in obese subjects, signalling excess stored energy. Leptin levels are also typically higher in women than men. So, when fasting, your leptin may decrease naturally, but mixed with sleep, healthy stress levels and feeding times could increase leptin levels in individuals. Therefore, eating less fatty food means there would be no need for leptin to increase. If you are intermittently fasting and eating the right foods, your leptin levels will stabilise, and you will be able to fast longer.

Ghrelin: Ghrelin is a hormone produced in the gastrointestinal tract, primarily the stomach, and is also known as the hunger hormone, regulating hunger levels in the body. Ghrelin levels are high before feeding and dip after as part of the energy balance regulator in synchronicity with leptin. Ghrelin is theorised to be instrumental in long-term body weight and is higher in people with more body weight compared to someone leaner. When fasting, ghrelin levels increase for energy intake (eating) to keep your body functional. Intermittent fasting is a natural and effective way to regulate ghrelin, especially when staying away from refined sugars and carbs. Conversely, protein and fibre are key signals to the brain regarding feeling full and reducing ghrelin levels in the stomach.

Adiponectin: Adiponectin is a protein hormone derived from adipocytes (fat cells). It is instrumental in regulating glucose, breaking down fatty acids and protecting the body from insulin resistance. An increase in adiponectin is key in diabetes prevention, and omega-3 is an essential nutrient to help increase adiponectin activity in the body. Adiponectin also has anti-inflammatory and immune response properties. During intermittent fasting, adiponectin increases, helping reduce LDL (bad cholesterol) and regulating the cytokine balance essential for immune cellular growth and response.

Conclusion

Intermittent fasting has tremendous effects on the body in a multitude of positive ways. This is great as abnormalities in hormones can cause severe chronic diseases such as type 1 and type 2 diabetes, thyroid issues, certain types of cancer and neurodegenerative disease. Intermittent fasting or prolonged water fasts of up to 72 hours can regulate the body's systems. Fasting will stabilise, neutralise, signal and stimulate metabolic processes to encourage the body back into homeostasis. Make sure you speak to a qualified nutritionist, physician or medical professional before attempting any form of fasting to make sure you can fast safely.

Chapter 3

What Is Nutrition?

Nutrition is how the body acquires proper nourishment through vitamins, minerals and other sources to grow and maintain life. In order to do this, the human body utilises nutrients to nourish the body and provide energy, metabolise, absorb and assimilate to sustain life. The word nourish comes from an old Latin word *nutrire*, which means to feed or take care of. Therefore, when we look at healthy eating, the priority becomes how our nutritional choices take care of us. Nutrition can be broken down into two types of nutritional groups made up of specific nutrients known as micro and macronutrients. Micronutrients are a mixture of vitamins and minerals necessary for major biological functions in the body and are needed in relatively small amounts. Micronutrients are so important that severe deficiencies can cause critical levels of poor health, leading to a physiological and psychological breakdown. Examples of micronutrients include minerals like iodine, selenium and zinc and vitamins such as vitamins A, B and C. Consequently, when looking at food selection, make sure you opt for dark, leafy greens, vegetables and fruits that have the most bioavailable micronutrients possible. Macronutrients are also a mixture of minerals and vitamins you need in relatively larger amounts in order for the body to function at optimal health. We can place macronutrients into seven classes: carbohydrates, protein, fats, dietary fibre, minerals, vitamins and water. Examples of macromineral vitamins and minerals include potassium, magnesium, phosphorus, and vitamins D, K and E are major minerals that mostly provide structural material (amino acids and lipids), so deficiencies in macrominerals can also create a critical condition for the body.

Origin of Nutrition

Nutrition is as old as humankind itself. Looking at anthropological data, we can see as far back as pre-history that we were in tune with our dietary needs, from the early hunter-gatherers who drank fresh water and ate seasonal grains, vegetables and, depending on ethnicity, buffalos, chicken, fish and other forms of meat. Around 400 BCE, Hippocrates, an ancient Greek physician termed the "Father of Medicine", proclaimed, "Let food be thy medicine". In reality, Hippocrates studied at the feet of the master in Kemet (modern Egypt) at the library of Alexandria, where the knowledge of the world was being held. Everything from disease, medicine and nutrition was accessible to students from all over the world.

Furthermore, we can look at the Ebers Smith Papyrus written by the polymath, chancellor and physician of the old Kemetic kingdom Imhotep. The diets of ancient Egypt provided a nutritious richness mainly comprising vegetables, wheat, nutritional beer, grains and lots of fruits. Ancient Egyptians knew that their spirituality was the key to life, extending to spiritual food, which was rather nutritious. Spiritual food refers to food that raises the vibration of the individual by providing balanced and adequate amounts of nutrition to strengthen the mind, body and emotional state. In pre-modern Europe, Asia and North Africa, the essential point of food was to directly influence health and well-being as an intricate part of a thriving society. For example, liver juices would have been used to treat a multitude of eye infections and diseases connected to a deficiency in vitamin

A. Other foods like garlic and ginger were used for boosting metabolism and strengthening the immune system.

Nutritional Science

Back in the mid-1700s, a physician in the British Navy by the name of Dr James Lind noticed that sailors on his ship were suffering from a vitamin C deficiency. This would typically take place on long voyages. He saw that these sailors ate primarily bread and meat. Consequently, Dr Lind developed an acute experiment by creating three study groups. He fed one group salt water, another he fed limes and the third, vinegar. The prognosis was that the group who were given limes did not develop scurvy due to the rich vitamin C levels. Despite the fact that vitamin C was not discovered explicitly until around the 1930s, it hugely transformed the way physicians understood the impact of food and created a new market for careers in nutrition.

Nutritional Behaviours & Beliefs

Food as we know it is a fundamental part of our societal structure. It holds symbolic cultural meaning and provides a historical roadmap telling you about the people of a society. In many ways, the food we eat in our societies can tell you a lot about the general health of the people and how they might be living. For example, if you live in the West, you will see that we consume huge amounts of salt, sugar and saturated fats. This explains the fact that our society has obesity problems that are compromising our health system and an increase in certain diseases, reaching epidemic levels. However, as societies evolve, adjustments are made, such as through health policies or even social media activists. Such individuals or groups push for change and want to open the dialogue via social media, advising people on what to do to improve their lives, which can influence food choices, such as the growing trend of veganism in the West. Generally speaking, when it comes to nutritional quality, there are various factors that determine food behaviour: values, religion, culture, environment and economics. How we assess these is down to what we eternalise from observing our childhood and what we have become accustomed to.

Food Behaviours

One of the most important factors regarding our acquired feeding habits has to do with how our parents raised us and how our social environment influenced us. Evaluating our early introduction to food places us in our early years of development, where we were exposed to specific types of nutrition and how sugar and salt played a major role in shaping our diet. So, if you were allowed an unadulterated amount of sugar due to social norms within your family structure, you might develop a sweet tooth, which will later become a very significant part of your life. If not accompanied by a balanced diet, it can result in serious health problems such as obesity, diabetes and other complex diseases. As we progress in age, we start to use food for emotional comfort and support to cope with the many stresses of life. We often turn to food that stimulates dopamine to provide biochemical relief in the brain so we can calm the neuroactivity in the amygdala that deals with fight or flight systems. We may also look at what we find easily accessible within our homes, which can either support healthy lifestyles or poor diet habits that lead to dysfunctional eating patterns like eating late, not drinking enough water or simply focusing on processed foods.

Food Addiction

The idea of food addiction has gained traction due to the huge number of scientific studies explaining how the foods we consume impact our physiology. The first thing we should know is that food is meant to simulate cellular growth, aid metabolism, provide energy and nourish the body. This is only achievable if we consume foods that are rich in minerals and vitamins. If we prioritise food with lower nutritional values, we will not be able to provide our bodies with adequate support to function optimally.

Food addiction is about impulsive habits that result in the mismanagement of food and, consequently, overindulging in low-nutritional food. Poor eating patterns can lead to excess weight, high blood pressure, diabetes, cardiovascular issues and other neurodegenerative diseases. When it comes to what fuels addiction, the brain is a great place to start biochemically. Various parts of the brain are stimulated when we eat, which triggers our innate survival behaviours. In other words, these various neuro-pathways exist so we can enjoy participating in basic survival activities such as eating. The part of the brain that influences choices for reward-related behaviour is called the "striatum", which is the largest part of your basal ganglia. When eating food that you enjoy, your amygdala is responsible for learning by absorbing new flavours you may like and remembering them every time you smell, see or taste them. This is why eating healthy can be a challenge, as you may already experience an overwhelming subconscious emotional connection to unhealthier options and junk food. In summary, you will struggle to say NO to bad food because your amygdala may be overwhelmed with a sense of pleasure. This response shuts down your rational thinking abilities, leading to the repetitive submission to food.

Signs of Food Addiction

Food addiction can easily go unnoticed. This is because it is normally woven into the fabric of the individual's personality. Every food choice or appetite is a mixture of emotional and psychological synchronicity that seamlessly influences how we eternalise our experiences, beliefs and expectations. Below are some tell-tale signs of possible food addiction:

- Eating way more than necessary
- Bingeing regularly on specific, particularly enjoyed foods
- Regularly eating until feeling physically sick
- Eating food that has already been recognised to not sit well in the stomach
- Going out of the way to obtain foods that are not readily accessible
- Filling time with food rather than being proactive
- Avoiding situations out of fear of certain foods being present
- Experiencing agitation and grumpiness without certain foods

Possible Solutions to Food Addiction

The first thing you need to do is realise that you have poor eating habits and that you have an unhealthy relationship with food. When you accept that, the key question to ask yourself is if you are willing to give up junk food. This is an extremely important question requiring sincere honesty and deep thought because, without this determination you will not make real change. Here are some solutions:

- Try 12-step programs for addiction because that's what it is: an addiction.
- Identify your trigger foods by keeping a food journal, and address them step by step.
- Hire a qualified nutritional therapist to help you understand the root cause and decide on bespoke steps to take together.
- Food displacement techniques where you shift those foods to designated days to allow control without giving up too much.
- Reduce bad carbs (white bread, white pasta, cakes, pastries) and increase protein and fibre-rich foods.

Religious Nutrition

Religion has influenced people's diets and eating patterns for as long as it has existed. Religion has deeply impacted the health and well-being of the people who subscribe to the principles and beliefs of each faith. Across many religions, food is associated with purification, nourishment or sacrifice. It seems to be a source or apparatus to gain a deep connection with the deity they serve. This is very important because there is a deep, innate connection between food consumption for the sustainability of life.

- **Buddhism:** Buddhists are predominantly vegans and vegetarians. Some may eat fish or consume dairy alongside fruits and vegetables, but fasting is an essential part for all. This is because Buddhists believe that food is for nourishment and essential to increase the vitality of the individual. Buddhists are encouraged not to attach themselves to the emotional aspect of food and incorporate fasting to focus on self-purification to reach enlightenment.
- **Judaism:** Jewish law dictates that its people should eat Kosher meals. Kosher food must be properly prepared by a trained person who has purified the food, making it suitable for consumption after the proper steps are taken under the tenets of Jewish law. Pork is strictly prohibited. Meat and dairy cannot be eaten together – waiting at least three hours to have dairy after meat. Eggs can be eaten as long as there are no blood spots, and fruits, vegetables and fasting are also essential to the practice.
- **Islam:** In Islam, the dietary standard can be split into two factions, Halal and Haram. Muslims will eat strictly Halal food (food which has been blessed and made permissible by evoking the name of Allah at the time it was killed or prepared). The other category, Haram food, is food that has not been properly prepared according to Islamic law. Pork is

strictly prohibited, while chicken, fish and all other animals must be halal. Dairy is permissible. Eggs, fruits, vegetables and fasting are all part of this dietary practice.

- **Christianity**: In Christianity, very few foods are prohibited, such as hooves, intestines and things of that nature, but this is not strictly enforced. Bread and wine are staples of Christian food because of the symbolic connection to Jesus. However, Christians are fairly free to eat anything as long as they are not a glutton for food. Consequently, fruit, vegetables, meat, fish, dairy, grains, bread and other things are allowed. Fasting for Lent is also widely encouraged as a day to observe the resurrection of the Lord.

Cultural Nutrition

Culturally, food holds symbols and meaning. As the great Dr Jessica Harris said, food provides a historical road map. Our initial introduction to food started with our social environment and how our parents or custodians prepared and consumed food daily. In your native environment, there is an innate relationship with food, from the time in your mother's stomach to how your early years of solid foods shaped your palette. These very same conditions in ancient times provided a symbiotic relationship between man and his food. This means that our habitats must provide the right amount of nutritional diversification to feed the people on the land. The key component of this relationship between man and food is gut bacteria. Gut bacteria are the microbes in the gut that play an essential role in human adaptation, immunity, nutritional absorption and metabolism. This gut flora ecosystem is created by innate prokaryotic and eukaryotic cells in your digestive tract. However, more studies have shown the origins of horizontal gene transfer in some eukaryotic cells. This means microbes exist that are not indigenous to the gut but are there by way of transmission. This is why travelling to a different environment may cause a person to experience difficulties eating certain local foods because of the difference in gut flora. Each culture has a staple diet that connects people to that environment and is symbolic of the people in that culture. I will provide some examples of cultural cuisines that speak to nutritional values typically represented in that region:

West African Nutrition: Across the continent, there are various types of cultural foods down to the many tribes within a nation. However, in West Africa, the nutritional landscape has evolved heavily. In ancient times, more fruit, vegetation and grains were staples in diets across the continent, but in the 21st century, this has shifted with the addition of cattle, dairy, chicken, seafood and a variety of meats. As nations developed and food industries expanded to feed the ever-growing population, tribes had to adapt new eating practices whilst retaining cultural essence. Rice, root vegetables, dairy, fruits, meat and a variety of grains are very common. Given the hard labour and beating sun, organic foods rich in protein, fibre and carbohydrates and primarily drinking water make for strong, resilient and creative people. However, due to lack of proper nutritional education, colonialism and poor practices, there are more cases of high blood pressure, strokes and obesity.

Western Nutrition: In Western diets, we can find every subgroup of cultural diet available because there is access to food groups from almost every part of the world. For example, in the UK, you can find Turkish foods, Indian foods, African foods (from different parts of Africa), Eastern European foods and so on. The staples of European diets are predominantly foods high in sugar and fats and are highly processed. There is also a culture of mass overconsumption. As much as we advocate for healthy eating in the West, the high statistical numbers on obesity, heart disease and high blood pressure are always alarming.

Sixty-three percent of people in the UK are overweight, and that's due to poor diet, education and habits.

Latin American Nutrition: In Latin America, food culture is so diverse, ranging from delicious vegetable dishes to meat-based dairy dishes. The primary reason for this diversity in cuisine is a result of African, Native American, European and Asian influences due to the historical influence of indigenous trade. You will find beans, meat, corn-based tacos, spices, menudo, pupusas, cassava, spinach, and so much more.

Cooking techniques from grilling in foil, deep frying, BBQ and steaming are all prevalent throughout the continent. One of the many benefits of the Latin American diet is how food is treated in their culture. Food is spiritual – it's about family, intermarriages and marking special occasions. It is a reflection of the efficient agricultural practices that make Latin food so rich and symbolic of their history. The continent also experiences mass poverty, making access to nutritional foods more difficult alongside socioeconomic problems. Modern nutrition includes a high use of starchy carbs, refined oils and a high glycaemic diet, causing more cases of hypertension, cardiovascular disease and diabetes.

Asian Nutrition: Typically, culture and spirituality play a massive role in the nutritional content of Asian cuisine. Asian cuisine has also become a staple in the West and is enjoyed by billions of people all over the world. China played a key role in supporting the globalisation of things like rice, broomcorn and foxtail millet. Despite the meat-based version of Asian food portrayed heavily in the West, a typical diet in China predominantly includes vegetables, small amounts of fish, poultry and, at times, red meat. General East Asian philosophies teach that nourishing the body, acquiring the right balanced nutrition and keeping the body strong are paramount to life. This is because Asian traditions are some of the most preserved traditions throughout the centuries, so food still represents divine intelligence as an intricate part of our physical existence and represents a deep, rich history and their people. Western influence in the major cities has changed the way Asian food is prepared and packaged. However, the simplicity of a root-based lifestyle makes for moderate eating with a balanced work lifestyle. The medicine-food-based understanding makes native Asian food balanced for consumption.

Environmental Nutrition

When we look at the state of health affairs of a country, we can be sure that food culture will be the basis of the overall day-to-day well-being of the people. Environmental nutrition deals with how we maintain steady physical and economic access to adequate nutritional foods to meet our dietary needs. Food security, along with a robust food supply system and a safe production standard, prevents mass hunger and diseases. However, social and political changes and global environmental changes threaten such success, ultimately hugely impacting food security. Food security typically looks at all of the necessary mechanics that provide constant access to safe food ready for consumption. Some key components include production, agriculture and packaging. A deep study into how we sustain an efficient food system requires us to broaden the conversation to the individual economics of people who have enough income to sustain a healthy diet as opposed to cheap, non-nutritional food. The bottom line is that everyone should be able to afford good quality food as a human right. For example, we can look at how the COVID-19 pandemic rendered many people jobless and struggling to feed their families. What would the long-term effects be of a large-scale shift in economic class? This will create an unequal world where people with low incomes can't afford healthy, nutritious food.

Current Economic Data

The reality is that eating healthy carries financial implications that make healthy living a challenge –almost impossible at times. Within the UK, it is very easy to see the uneven distribution of whole foods stores and fast-food chains throughout different areas. For example, low-income areas have families living in poverty with multiple fast-food restaurants close by, serving very unhealthy processed foods. However, more affluent areas have a diverse layout of whole food stores, fresh juice bars and a much better balance of healthy food.

https://www.ons.gov.uk/peoplepopulationandcommu   nity/ personalandhouseholdfinances/expenditure/   bulletins/ familyspendingintheuk/april2019tomarc h2020

Average Food Costs per Month

- **Per Person:** The average monthly food budget in the UK is £175 per person, of which £115 is spent on grocery shopping and £60 on food prepared outside the home, such as takeaways and restaurant meals.
- **Average Adult Man:** The average adult male would spend around £140 on groceries and £72 on food out, £212 altogether on food each month.
- **Young, Active Adult Man:** A young, active adult man around 18 years of age whose caloric needs are 50% higher than the average person would theoretically spend around £262 a month on food (£173 on groceries and £89 out).
- **Average Adult Woman:** The average adult female would spend around £107 on groceries and £55 on food out, adding up to £162 altogether on food each month.
- **Young, Active Adult Woman:** A young, active adult woman around 18 years of age whose caloric needs are 13% higher

than the average person would theoretically spend around £198 a month on food (£130 on groceries and £67 out).

- **Two Adults:** The total food budget for two adults in the UK is twice this, or £374 per month – £246 on groceries and £128 on eating out.

- **Family of Three:** The average food bill for a family of three (with two adults and one younger child) in the UK is around £514 per month – £339 of which is spent on grocery shopping and £175 on eating out.

- **Family of Four:** The average UK family of four (two adults and two younger children) spends £654 in total on food each month – £431 on grocery shopping bills and another £223 on food out.

- **Family of Five:** Larger families of five (two adults and three younger children) spend around £523 a month on groceries and another £271 on food out, bringing the total average food bill for a family of five to around £794.

- **Family of Three Adults:** Three adults (or two adults and an older teenage child) would spend around £369 on groceries, £191 on food prepared and £561 altogether on food each month, clearly with budgets varying by the age and gender of the family members.

Conclusion

With the average household income being around £2,000 per month (according to statista.com), those below the poverty line would struggle to afford the cost of living, let alone afford healthy foods that are way above the average cost of junk food. The average cost of healthy eating per day is around £7.68 compared to £2.48 per day to eat junk food. You can see the gap that makes it almost impossible for low-income houses to afford a healthy, sustainable lifestyle. The key thing to remember is healthy eating is one part, but healthy living is holistic. Consequently, there are basic things we can do every day to help get more out of healthy living, such as exercise, good sleep, drinking lots of water and adding more vegetables to your diet. You can reduce your sugar intake, cook more instead of ordering out and avoid over consuming by adding structure and control to your diet.

Nutritional Genetics

Innovative research has helped scientists get a better understanding of the effects of nutrition on your genes. This is called nutrigenomics, and it focuses on the relationship between food and DNA. Thanks to our richer understanding of epigenetics, we can observe how our genes respond to several environmental influences. In this case, nutrition is an environmental factor that directly affects gene expression, such as Folate, Vitamin A and Vitamins B2, B6 and B12. Another example is how specific diets, such as a high glycaemic diet (foods that spike blood sugar), directly modulate the adiponectin gene, contributing to the development of insulin resistance that causes type 2 diabetes. Even metabolic processes are a result of genetic coding that impacts enzyme activity, receptors, proteins and hormones in our body. Consequently, the food you eat will directly impact important things such as growth, ageing and susceptibility to non-communicable diseases. This is great for us to understand that our food choices have deep genetic consequences and, therefore, allows us to have a deeper view of how food impacts our health.

Epigenetics

Epigenetics is about understanding how environmental factors impacting our genes are expressed. In this instance, we will look at the science of how our food selection affects people's varied nutrition and impacts our DNA. There are two major factors in how the process of gene expression via epigenetics works: methylation and histone proteins that provide chromatic structure to DNA. Put simply, methylation is about the addition of a methyl group as part of gene silencing by the replacement of a hydrogen atom. When methylation works, it can silence a cancer-causing gene, and when we ingest processed foods or alcohol, methylation fails to work properly and causes development issues. Histones are proteins that allow the DNA to wrap around and fit into the nucleus. Some of its key roles are to prevent DNA damage, play a major part in gene expression and regulate DNA replication. These are very important processes that take place, especially as it relates to food. Eating processed foods or food with a high glycaemic index (food that pushes blood sugar up) will significantly negatively affect histones and the methylation process. This is how we develop conditions such as type 2 diabetes, cardiovascular problems, fibroids, obesity, and so much more.

Nutritional Markers

Epigenetic markers essentially do not change DNA sequences or re-arrange them in any way, so your inherited DNA from your parents remains intact. Epigenetic markers, such as methylation, affect local chromatin environments and thus affect how DNA is expressed. These same markers help turn genes on and off depending on what we are actually eating. Contrary to your fixed DNA sequence, these epigenetic markers undergo various changes in response to your cell cycle as part of cellular generation for survival. Specific alterations of epigenetic markers can be passed on to the next generation or a type of modulation of specific gene groups that can potentially lead to disease. So if you have a particular diet, you can pass markers for obesity or diabetes on to your children. However, this does not mean that your offspring will definitely experience the same fate. Rather, it means they have the potential, based on their own nutritional development, to bring about these conditions that can become a real problem.

Healing (A Balanced Lifestyle)

In reality, scientists, nutritionists, dieticians and your local general practitioner cannot all agree on a specific diet that's best for all of the issues that our society deals with today. What we can agree on is the fact that nutrition has requirements. We need over 114 nutrients every day to meet our daily requirements for optimal health.

Consequently, I can only arrive at one word that moves the needle to the exact point of discussion needed to move us forward in the science of nutrition. That word is **balanced,** which is the key to everything when it comes to how we define health. Health is about the absence of disease or physical impairment, keeping up with life's basal daily demands and finding an inner balance between yourself and your environment. So, the question is: How does one achieve a balanced and healthy lifestyle? The human body needs several key elements to produce an emotional, physiological and psychological stable person. First, let's start with how you structure your meals based on nutritional requirements to give the body sufficient energy and the benefit of anti-inflammatory properties. Half your plate (50%) should be a mixture of colourful vegetables and leafy greens, 25% protein and 25% whole-grain carbs. Adding 2–3 litres of water daily is also essential (this can include herbal teas). Healthy fats and a range of fruits will complete your meal plan for the day. Aside from diet, which is only 25% of health, exercise is 25%, sleep/rest is 25%, and the other 25% should be based on mindfulness, meditation and developing your mental wellness.

- **Importance of sleep:** Sleep is one of the most powerful tools we have to keep our body functional and healthy. Sleep is part of a circadian rhythm cycle that allows the body's internal body clock to sync with day and night. Melatonin, the key hormone required for sleep, is secreted by the pineal gland and allows the body to perform a plethora of important functions necessary for life. Sleep improves attention span and learning/memory, reduces stress levels, keeps the heart healthy, boosts the immune system, maintains a healthy weight, aids development and cellular repair, and so many other biological functions, such as removing waste from the body. If you do not get enough sleep, you can disturb the body's equilibrium, causing mental or psychological issues, emotional problems and ageing. In summary, no matter how you look at it, sleep is essential for health and any form of recovery, so make sure you get enough of it.

- **Exercise is necessary:** Exercise is key to mental, physical and emotional well-being. Fundamentally, exercise is about improving oxygen efficiency by increasing lung capacity, heart strength and muscle motility. Exercising regularly at least five days per week would be best, combining weights, resistance and cardio. Some amazing benefits of exercise include a healthy heart, lowering cholesterol levels, building strong muscles, building stronger bones, lowering blood pressure, maintaining a healthy weight and reducing stress in the body. Exercise is also essential for improving mood, and several studies show a major difference in people who suffer from anxiety or depression when they begin to exercise more regularly.

- **Importance of water:** Water is made up of one hydrogen atom accompanied by two oxygen molecules. Water is essential for life. Our body is approximately 60% water molecules, and it is essential we get a sufficient amount of water to stay hydrated. We typically need anywhere between 2.5–3 litres a day to make sure the body gets enough water to help with cellular health, brain function, heart function, skin health, proper digestion, optimal eye function, and so much more. The average adult in the UK is dehydrated because most drink well below their daily requirements. Children and the elderly are at the most risk of not consuming enough water on a day-to-day basis due to several factors, such as high sugar intake, physical access, etc. Typically, an older adult will hold up to 15% less water than a younger adult, so drinking more fluids, especially as you age, is very important.

- **Mental health:** Mental health has become a hot topic and rightfully a focus of our civilisation as we learn more and more about mental health problems. There are amazing studies that directly link diet to mental health and vice versa. When we talk about how gut health is linked to brain health, it's because it is said that 97% of serotonin is made in the gut (the same area you absorb nutrients in the body), and it's the way food impacts neurotransmitters to influence mood. For example, junk food like a chocolate bar may be rich in sugar and have no nutritional value. It will add to your anxiety by causing blood sugar levels to eventually crash and anxiety levels to spike because your mood is disrupted. One of the key parts of recovery from anxiety, depression and other mental disorders is eating a balanced diet to help balance the body.

Chapter 4

John Henryism

What we have learned over the years as a civilisation is that stress is a silent killer that contributes to some of the most common diseases in the world. Chiefly, cardiovascular diseases, to be more specific, because of how stress affects hypertension, which ultimately links to the heart's well-being. We know that high blood pressure significantly impacts all ethnic groups but is specifically prevalent among African and Caribbean people in the diaspora. In the US, African Americans are 2–4 times more likely to develop hypertension by age 50, and Black British citizens are 3–4 times more likely. We have hypothesised that multiple variable factors contribute to the excess risk to people of colour. We now understand that numerous environmental factors, genetics and socioeconomic status also play a massive role (socioeconomic factors refer to a person's education, occupation and financial situation). Even though generally speaking, these factors have a profound effect on Black and white people, there is an undeniable psychological factor that comes from general living conditions and interactions with the prevailing society that seems to increase susceptibility to cardiovascular problems. In the early 1970s, there were multiple studies that demonstrated that sustained mental engagement, accompanied by psychological stressors, led to a significant increase in systolic blood pressure. Berkman and Syme (1979) postulated that a person (especially a Black person) of lower socioeconomic status typically faces more stressful environmental stressors in contrast to people with more socioeconomic power. In conclusion, constant mental stressors within psychologically harsh environmental conditions over a long period of time may be the reason for the specific correlation between socioeconomic status and an increase in cardiovascular disease amongst Black people.

"John Henryism describes the stressful, damaging health impact of thriving despite inequality, financial hardship and racial discrimination".

Sherman James PHD

What Is John Henryism?

In the 1970s, an African American doctor by the name of Sherman James was investigating the racial health link between working conditions in the South. Later, he hypothesised that deep psychological stressors under prolonged socioeconomic impairment had a profound cardiovascular impact on Black people. The story of man versus machine goes as follows: John Henry was a Black railroad worker in the 1800s whose determination and strength were pushed to the limit, and it eventually killed him. John Henry's job was to create openings in rocks for explosives by hammering metal rods into the rocks. One day, the livelihood of the workers was threatened by advancements in industrial technology – a steam power drill. John Henry was then pitted against the machine in order to save hundreds of jobs, and unbelievably, he beat the machine. John Henry worked tirelessly, pushing his mental, emotional and physical capacity to the limits. John Henry won and beat the machine, but it eventually cost him his life. This epic man-against-machine contest inspired songs, books, films and even Dr James, whose research was all about the racial health disparities. In the 1970s, the epidemiologist Dr James also came across a man whose life had a resemblance to John Henry's life and even remarkably shared the name and went by John Henry Martin. John Henry Martin was an African American farmer in the rural South, born in poverty and also had his fight against the "machine" – systematic racism. After teaching himself how to read and write, John Henry Martin ended up owning 75 acres of land. John Henry Martin was very determined to clear his debt in five years by relentlessly working night and day. By his 50s, John Henry Martin suffered from multiple illnesses, such as high blood pressure, arthritis, and a peptic ulcer that was so bad he had to have 40% of his stomach removed. Consequently what we learn is that overworking the body with tremendous stress can lead to illness and eventually death.

Biological Impact of Psychological Stress

- **Musculoskeletal system**: When you are in stressful situations, the body will respond by tensing up the muscles as a way of self-defence from injury or pain. So, for example, if you are experiencing sudden stress, the muscles in your body will tense up and relax once the stressful situation has passed. Therefore, if you suffer from chronic stress, your muscles are in a constant state of tenseness, and over a prolonged period of time, this will lead to other chronic stress-related disorders. Another way to demonstrate this point is to look at two different tension types: headaches and migraines. Both tension types are often linked to prolonged muscular tension in the head, shoulders and neck. Other musculoskeletal pain often experienced in the lower back region has been associated with stress, especially job-related stress. However, many effective relaxation techniques and therapeutic remedies are available to help reduce muscle tension. Such methods include hydrotherapy using hot baths with magnesium salts to help relax muscles, acupuncture to stimulate sensory nerves by the strategic placement of needles around the body and massage therapy, where soft tissue is displaced to stimulate electrical signals to reduce pain.

- **Respiratory System:** A key function of the respiratory system is supplying oxygen to red blood cells to carry around the body. Experiencing strong emotions in the form of stress can cause shortness of breath and rapid breathing. This is because the airways in our nasal passage and lungs tighten to respond to the stress to guard the body. If you have any form of acute respiratory disease or any other respiratory problems, psychological stressors can become very problematic and make struggling to breathe fatal at times, such as severe asthma attacks. There have been a few compelling studies that convey how acute stressful events, such as losing a loved one, can trigger an asthma attack alongside hyperventilation, especially someone inclined to panic attacks. There are things you can do to remedy this, such as working with a therapist, counselling and using breathing techniques to help you calm yourself down and reduce the stress of the experience. In fact, learning deep slow breaths are one of the most successful ways to ease your heart rate and calm down the tension in the muscles, even if the environmental stressors are still actively present. This allows you to focus and think clearly enough to remove yourself or deal with the situation more effectively.

- **Cardiovascular System:** The cardiovascular system is key to pumping oxygenated blood throughout the body whilst filtering out carbon dioxide to keep your body in perfect rhythm to sustain life. When you are experiencing acute stress (on a short-term basis), such as arriving somewhere important late, getting stuck in traffic, or slamming the brakes in the car to prevent a potential accident, it can cause an increased heart rate. This causes more intense contractions within the heart muscle, and stress hormones like cortisol and epinephrine respond as messengers to these stressful situations. The blood vessels also dilate, which can cause an increased amount of blood flow to be pumped to the large muscles and heart. This is how your blood pressure increases. When put in these situations over a long period of time consistently, we start to see people developing hypertension or having heart attacks and strokes if they do not find balance or professional help. In summary, if you are working hard at work to survive, mixed with the constant environmental stresses of everyday life, not finding a balance will drive your body into succumbing to the aforementioned chronic diseases.

- **Gastrointestinal System:** With hundreds of millions of neurons in the gut transmitting directly to the brain, it is safe to say your gut is your second brain. With key neurotransmitters such as serotonin (the mood hormone) made predominantly in the gut, what we feel from our external environment will also be experienced in the gut. Stress can interfere with brain–gut communication and present major discomforts in the form of bloating, pain or constipation. When dealing with stress – especially long-term, chronic stress – the millions of gut bacteria that can influence brain and gut health will start to impact your cognitive functions and can cause low moods.

Conclusion

Stress is everyone's enemy and should be avoided at all costs. Regardless of ethnicity, stress impacts our bodies fundamentally the same, even when we factor in other variables, such as gender, age and environment. We can see why it's one of the biggest silent killers of our health. A balanced diet, exercise, fresh air, quality sleep and emotionally safe environments will be the cure for how we return to Eden. This is our mission, and when we start to deal with John Henryism, we realise that it's the working class and how they internalise their experiences that start to significantly deteriorate our quality of life. John Henryism brings about good conscience, an intellectually effective way to highlight the way we overexert ourselves to receive the same equal safety and protection. The key takeaway is that there is a deep, well-researched link between low socioeconomic status and cardiovascular conditions. This means we have to educate people and do a better job of making healthy, fresh food more available to everyone – regardless of socioeconomic status.

The Science of Water

Water is a universal substance composed of H_2O (one hydrogen with two oxygen atoms attached). Water has three commonly known states, which are gas, liquid, solid, but a 4th phase was discovered by Dr Pollock called EZ (exclusion zone water), also known as structured water. Water is an odourless, tasteless liquid at room temperature and can dissolve, move, create, transport and transform based on temperature and content due to its innate versatility. The general belief is that biological life as we know it originated from water, and all living organisms depend on water for them to exist. A belief in many indigenous cultures aligns with the prevailing scientifically accepted theory that the majority of the water on Earth came from outside our solar system originally. Modern science says that our water may have come from passing asteroids and solar nebulas. Our ancestors in the Dogon spiritual system on creation speak of Amma's egg being impregnated by the Nommos to convey hydrogen particles colliding with a formless earth without atmospheric conditions to create life. Scientists also claim that water has been found to exist on other neighbouring planets, including the moon, which has given scientists a lot of data on how potential life could possibly exist. Although water is colourless in relatively small amounts, it is said that water has an intrinsic blue colour in vast quantities (such as the ocean) due to the absorption of red wavelengths of light.

Water in the Body

The general scientific consensus says that 60% of the human adult body is made up of water.

According to H. H. Mitchell, Journal of Biological Chemistry, the lungs are about 83% water, muscles and kidneys are 79% water, the brain and heart are about 73% water, skin is about 64% water, and even bones are 31% water. In the human body, water performs four major important roles to sustain life: It acts like a transportation vehicle, a medium for chemical reactions, a lubricant or shock absorber, and a temperature regulator.

Water Transportation

Water is known as a universal solvent because it dissolves more substances than any other fluid known to man. These substances or "water solutes" in the human body include ions, sugar, amino acids, minerals and vitamins. The water molecules' hydrogen and oxygen can loosely bond with other agents, allowing water to be such a good solvent. Water properties allow easy transportation within the body because blood is the primary transport vehicle in the body, and blood is made up of mostly water. There are several dissolved substances within blood, such as protein, glucose, electrolytes, lipoproteins, urea and carbon dioxide, which are all metabolic waste products. All of these dissolve in the watery surroundings of blood to support basic cellular function through transportation. Without the water and its properties, your body would be unable to facilitate basic transportation needs for inter-cellular relations to support life.

Water as a Medium

In the most fundamental chemical reactions, water plays an intrinsic role, acting as a medium by either creating the right environment for enzymes or maintaining electrical balance in cells. Similarly, the medium in the human body that allows a multitude of chemical reactions to take place is water. Other essential benefits of water as a medium for chemical reactions are that water can store heat, has a neutral PH balance and is electrically neutral. Water also acts as an agent to help break down bonds in other molecules, and enzymes can operate freely and conduct necessary functions in the body in the medium of water. This is essential because without water acting as that critical medium, none of the essential chemical reactions needed for homeostasis would work, and thus, the human body would be unable to survive.

Water as a Lubricant and Shock Absorber Water is the main component of the fluids that protect and lubricate the body's systems. Fluids surrounding the brain, eyes and nerve cells act like a buffer in case of a change in the environment. For example, within the body, there are interstitial fluids made up of predominantly water surrounding cells and organs for both mechanical and chemical protection. Another example is how water fills the amniotic sac a few weeks after egg fertilisation to provide a safe environment for the developing embryo. Here are other important examples of the key role of water as both lubricant and shock absorber:

- The watery fluid surrounding the brain and spinal cord will act as a buffer for these organs in external environmental movements and changes.
- Synovial fluid lubricates joints and makes motility smoother and less painful.
- Two-layer membranes cover the lungs, acting as lubrication to allow the lungs to move with each breath, making breathing more functional.
- Fluid secretions in the digestive tract ease the passage of material such as faeces through the colon and small intestines.

Water as a Thermal Regulator

Water is a key component in the body's temperature regulation. The human body has a distinct set point of around 37° Celsius or 98.6° Fahrenheit. When body temperature drops too low or rises too high, enzymes in the body stop functioning properly, and metabolism is impaired. In the extreme scenario of your body temperature dropping to 28° Celsius, the nervous system would break down, and hypothermia would kick in, which can lead to muscle failure and potentially death. However, water has a stable heat capacity, which means water in the body is very efficient at storing heat and maintaining the body's set temperature at 37° Celsius, regardless of the environment's changing temperature. A great demonstration of how this mechanism occurs is how when you get cold, your skin signals your hypothalamus to help the body generate heat in different ways. One of the ways the hypothalamus does this is to signal smooth muscle tissues to constrict blood flow to reduce heat loss from the body. Another interesting way is how the hypothalamus stimulates the thyroid to secrete hormones that speed up metabolism and increase heat conversion to keep you warm.

Does the PH of Water Matter?

This is an age-old conversation that needs to be addressed across the board, and hopefully, more research will arise and give us a more practical way to utilise this. The first thing we need to look at is what the PH levels of water mean, how your body benefits, how much of it we should be drinking to make a significant impact, and what the research actually says. When we talk about alkaline water, we are talking about water with a PH of 8 or 9. There is a lot of anecdotal evidence, including claims of boosting immunity, clearing skin, regulating the body's PH and so forth. My professional perspective is that alkaline water by itself can be helpful in medicinal situations, such as acid reflux and IBS, where PH balance needs to be restored. However, I do not recommend alkaline water at a PH of 8 or 9 at 2.5 litres per day because of the risk of diluting your gut acid, which is key for digestion. We still have multi-variable factors, such as age, gender, ethnicity, health conditions, temperature and water absorption capacity, to give us a definite outlook on the best way to consume alkaline water. Anecdotal evidence is a claim a person has made based on their experiences on a personal level, taking it as fact, and that can often be confusing for the average person looking for scientific truth. My research has shown me that alkaline water seems very effective for 3–4 months at 2 litres a day for specific conditions, such as digestive issues or acid reflux. Outside of these parameters, drinking 2–3 litres of water per day is the general recommended intake but can vary from person to person. The most important principle to remember is that the body requires balance, and the water in your body has a neutral PH7. If you over consume alkaline water, there are some adverse effects, such as reducing the stomach's natural acidity, which is instrumental in destroying bacteria as well as restricting certain ingested pathogens from hitting your bloodstream. Consequently, the conversation becomes about overconsumption and how much is too much. I strongly recommend that you seek professional advice from trained dieticians, nutritionists or your general practitioner regarding any diet change involving alkaline water consumption.

Best Types & Ways to Consume Water

Everyone has a preference for water depending on taste and the vitality that they experience. The best type of water, hands down, is contaminant-free, clean, pure water. This type of water is the benchmark for how humans should consume water, and with these points, water can be deemed safe to drink. However, here are some basic and generally accepted ways to consume water:

- Have a glass of water covered at your bedside to drink first thing in the morning to replace all the fluids lost in the night.
- Set reminders on your phone to drink water every two hours throughout the day.
- Multiple studies have determined that room-temperature water is best for you.
- Adding lemon or ginger can increase the body's water absorption.
- It has been recommended to drink slowly rather than in big gulps.

10 Benefits of Water

1. Water Helps Create Saliva
    Saliva is mainly composed of water and small amounts of electrolytes, enzymes and mucus. Saliva plays a crucial role in digestion in the mouth by breaking down solids for the stomach and keeping your mouth healthy and functional. The more water you drink, the healthier your saliva glands operate.

2. Water Helps Sweat, Bowel Movements & Kidney Function
    In order to sweat, urinate or even have bowel movements, your body will utilise water to make these components functional. The more water you drink, the easier it is for the kidneys to filter out urea, for your body to push out sweat and allow bowel movements to progress more smoothly.

3. Water Can Improve Physical Performance
    Drinking water during physical activities, especially exercise, can help boost strength, power and endurance. You could easily dehydrate yourself whilst playing or participating in strenuous physical

activities over a period of time. Adequate hydration allows the muscles, heart and lungs to function better.

4. Water Can Help with Nutrient Absorption
   Water helps break down food whilst dissolving water-soluble vitamins and minerals from your food. It also transports vitamin components throughout your body.

5. Water Can Help You Lose Weight
   Drinking more water can help reduce calorie intake as most people are dehydrated and often confuse thirst for hunger. Water intake can increase resting rate expenditure, and it has been said that drinking cold water can force the body to use up more calories to heat it up to body temperature.

6. Water Can Improve Blood Oxygen Circulation Water is key in the transportation of oxygen around the body, and drinking the recommended daily allowance can improve circulation. This is very important because it means organs, muscles and bones are healthier because of adequate circulation and nutrients get utilised around the body more efficiently.

7. Water Can Help Fight Off Illness
   If we are dehydrated, our bodies won't be able to effectively remove toxins from cells and keep cells healthy. Also, dehydration has a significant effect on the innate immune system.

8. Water Can Boost Energy
   Drinking enough water can ramp up your metabolism to help you utilise energy and give you the boost you need. Studies have shown that drinking water regularly boosts your metabolic rate by 30%.

9. Water Improves Mood
    Water can even improve mood and reduce anxiety and agitation to calm down nerves. Dehydration increases stress in the body, and it takes sufficient amounts of water to create serotonin, and not enough serotonin can result in depression.

10. Water Helps Keep Skin Healthy
    Sufficient daily water intake has a significant impact on skin health by aiding collagen production. Even though water alone won't slow down ageing, you retain less water as you age, so consuming water will help the skin's PH balance and remove toxins, amongst other things, to keep your skin looking great.

Dehydration and Symptoms

Dehydration is when your body uses more fluid than you're able to consume. Given the many significant functions of water and its key roles, not having enough water can be detrimental to human biology. The average adult in the UK drinks about 1.5–1.7 litres of water per day, which is well under the daily recommended consumption of 2.5–3 litres. Statistically, one in four people actually drink the recommended daily consumption, which also means many people have acute or chronic health issues tied to their lack of water intake in some way or another.

Chronic dehydration can often result in a number of serious complications, including:

*   Swelling in your brain
*   Kidney failure
*   Seizures
*   Headaches
*   Being unable to focus or concentrate

- Passing darker urine than usual
- Tiredness or fatigue
- Muscle weakness and cramps
- Constipation
- Dry, flaky skin
- Altered kidney, heart or digestive function

Conclusion

The bottom line is that water is key for life and should not be taken lightly. With so much access to water in the West, it has always astounded me how little of it we drink. Now, a lot of this is cultural as well as educational, in the sense that we need to educate children from the start on the importance of water as well as information about water and its impact on health. Many of us did not grow up prioritising water, and even if we did, the major corporations have spent billions on advertising sugar drinks to us to the point where it's the preferred or default option. When you are thirsty, your body is signalling you for more water, not fizzy, high-sugar drinks. These sugary drinks do not quench thirst or provide the body with what it needs, and if you are addicted to drinking such things, try your best to educate yourself and develop healthier habits around water intake.

The Science of Herbs

Herbalists use medicinal plants and herbs to help change the body's biochemistry to create a harmonious balance and wellness within the body. In reality, herbs are far more suited to and in alignment with the body as opposed to isolated chemicals from pharmaceutical medicine. With around 70,000 plant species ranging from tall, towering trees to short basil leaves, herbal medicine has been at work for centuries. Most herbs used on a regular basis are deemed extremely safe for medicinal use, but some plants can cause side effects and, just like any other medicine, should be treated with great respect. When dealing with herbal plants, it is generally advised to take them under the guidance of trained professional herbalists who can safely recommend doses and correct preparation. For example, the herbal plant ephedra can have adverse effects when taken at the wrong dosage and can even be extremely toxic.

Ancient Herbalism

In classical history, we see the past importance of the medicinal plants that have provided human beings with sustainable health and general well-being. For example, flaxseed, also known as *linum usitatissimum,* has been used as a nutritious food oil, in cosmetic balms and medicinally to treat acute respiratory illnesses and several digestive problems. Around 3,000 BCE onwards, we see the ancient civilisations of China, India and Egypt advanced in traditional medicine with a more sophisticated application of herbal medicine. Some of the earliest recorded mentions of herbal remedies can be found in the Ebers Smith Papyrus, where Kemetic polymath Imhotep makes reference to the use of herbal remedies and lists them and their relationship with spells and incantations. In India, the Vedas (c.1500 BCE) contains rich literature on the herbal lore of that time, which was used well into 500 BCE. Around 500 BCE, we see herbalism begin to separate itself from the world of magic and mysticism. Hippocrates (460–377 BCE), the Greek "Father of Medicine", started to explore the idea that sickness was a natural response to both the external and internal environment rather than superstition followed by a magical event. He also postulated that medicine was effective due to its own constituents, and there was no need to accompany treatment with ritualistic ceremonies or blood sacrifices.

How Medicinal Plants Work

In extreme situations, such as a traumatic injury caused by a freak accident or some unexplained occurrences, there is no doubt that modern medicine has an unparalleled opportunity to save lives or reduce symptoms for more comfort. Herbal medicines are explicitly different from pharmaceutical drugs. A typical plant will house different bioactive phytocompounds in the thousands, and when combined into tinctures, can have even more compounds. These compounds and constituents are the active chemicals in the plant that help reduce inflammation or starve parasites in the body. Herbs are still an equivocal part of healing and can play an exclusive role or act as an alternative if access to modern medicine is unavailable.

A great example of this was found in a newspaper article back in 1993 in the capital city of Bosnia, where a war-torn hospital could not receive its regular medicinal supplies and had to end up using valerian as an anaesthetic and pain killer. Valerian herb is far more equipped to deal with anxiety and nervous tensions in the body but could at least calm the injured down enough to buy time for proper treatment to be administered.

Regardless of where one may stand, herbalism has a lot to offer, and up to the 1800s, humans have had to rely primarily on herbal remedies to survive.

A Few Active Constituents in Herbs

- **Phenols:** These are a specific group of anti-inflammatory and antiseptic elements, which consist of a range of constituents from salicylic acid (a molecule similar to aspirin) to phenolic glycosides, which plants produce to fight off infection and keep insects from feeding on the plant. Many plants in the mint family also contain phenols, making them strong antioxidants with effective antiseptic properties. A great demonstration of phenols is peppermint oil. When used in a diffuser, it can greatly help sanitise the atmosphere. It is very effective for people suffering from hay fever, sinus problems or the common cold.

- **Flavonoids:** These polyphenolic compounds are found throughout the plant world and act as a pigment – mostly yellow or white in fruits and vegetables. They are a very effective ingredient when it comes to anti-inflammatory properties and are very effective in improving circulation in the body. Hesperidin and rutin are flavonoids found in lemon or buckwheat, as well as a plethora of other plants. These flavonoids are great when it comes to strengthening capillaries to prevent leakage into other surrounding tissues.

- **Volatile Oils:** These are a group of oils distilled from plants to produce essential oils and are the most useful constituents in many different situations to help healing. These volatile oils are also a popular constituent used in perfumery, mostly made up of a hundred or more compounds, such as monoterpenes (molecules containing ten or more carbon atoms). These volatile oils are used in aromatherapy, massage oils, or to be evaporated in diffusers, such as tea tree oils. Volatile oils are also often used in foods, drinks and household cleaning products to add scent.

- **Tannins:** These are polyphenolic micronutrients derived from plants that contract and pull together the tissues, such as those used in anti-ageing creams or to replenish skin and bring back vitality to the body by binding precipitating proteins. Tannins containing herbs are used to tighten up loose or relaxed tissue caused by varicose veins and reduce excessive water secretion to help alleviate diarrhoea symptoms. Examples of herbs and foods with tannins include strawberries, cranberries, blueberries, apricots, mints, dry fruits, cloves, hibiscus, witch hazel and shepherd's purse.

- **Saponins:** These are the active water- and fat-soluble constituents used to make soap. Saponins come in two forms: steroidal and triterpenoid. Saponins are mostly derived from soapwort. When properly prepared under the guidance of a well-trained herbalist, it can be great for skin, lowering blood glucose and as an anti-viral. Plants that contain saponins are protected against all forms of microbial attacks, such as fungi.

- **Cardiac glycosides:** These plant-based compounds are found in the bark of wild cherries, apricots and other fruits. They are often rich in antioxidants and, in small doses, have a sedative, relaxant effect on the heart. Cardiac glycosides are often used to treat heart conditions but also have anti-cancer, anti-inflammatory and anti-tumour properties. If the right dose is not taken, the potential adverse effects include dizziness, headache, anxiety, stomachache, change in taste and potential blurred vision.

- **Anthraquinones:** These are a multi-use organic compound found in plants that can be used for dye, pigment and medicinal uses.

- Anthraquinones are the key ingredient in herbs like senna that help relieve constipation. Anthraquinones have a laxative effect on the colon walls by inducing a bowel movement ten hours after consumption and softening stool. Some foods containing anthraquinones include rhubarb root, senna leaf, cascara and buckhorn.

- **Alkaloids:** These are a group of nitrogen-based organic compounds that are a by-product of plant metabolism. Alkaloids aid in metabolic growth in plants, but therapeutically, they can be used as an anaesthetic, possess cardioprotective properties, and have intrinsic anti-inflammatory properties when used medicinally. Some examples of alkaloids that we are very familiar with include morphine, ephedrine and nicotine. Examples of foods that contain alkaloids include potatoes, eggplants, tomatoes, coffee beans and tea leaves, to name a few.

- **Bitters:** These are a variety of constituents sourced from specific bark, roots and herbs. They are linked only by their bitter taste, which stimulates salivary glands and digestive organs. It improves the absorption quality of nutrients in the body, providing an amazing effect on the digestive system. Furthermore, bitters can help relieve indigestion, nausea, heartburn and stomach cramps and can be found in wormwood herbs, watercress, horseradish and other plants. You can use bitters ten minutes before food or after a night of overeating to help ease any digestive side effects.

List Of Herbs

1. For Constipation & Diarrhoea

- **Yellow Dock**: Mild laxative.
- **Senna**: Strong laxative.
- **Psyllium husk/seeds:** Act as a colon cleanser and help with diarrhoea.
- **Cramp Bark**: Helps with spastic constipation due to its antispasmodic properties (compounds that modulate smooth contractions in the GI tract).
- **Agrimony**: An herb that's great for helping to ease diarrhoea.

Diet For Constipation: Eating fresh fruits daily, such as berries, peaches, apricots, plums, figs, rhubarb, and prunes. Make sure you're hitting your 2.5 litres of water daily.

2. Nerve Pain

- **St John's Wort:** With its anti-inflammatory properties, St John's Wort is very effective in treating neuralgia and sciatica pain by soothing irritated nerves. It even helps regenerate nerve tissue.

- **Clove:** Clove acts as a natural anaesthetic by numbing nerve cells and can be very useful for dental nerve pain.
- **Peppermint:** Helps muscles relax and controls muscle spasms to help relieve pain with its anti-inflammatory properties.
- **Cayenne Pepper:** The main ingredient, capsaicin, is very effective on the sensory nerves and helps with minor pain from muscle sprains and rheumatoid arthritis.

Diet For Nerve Pain: Eating lots of leafy greens and vegetables containing B vitamins will help aid in nerve generation and healing. Foods rich in vitamins B1, B6 and B12, to be exact, are best to manage nerve pain.

3. Skin Problems

- **Witch Hazel:** With the leaves and tiny twigs being the key component of these herbs, they can be very powerful anti-inflammatory agents with astringent properties, which means they can reduce redness and skin sores and make the skin tight and vibrant again. It can be used for rashes, cysts, spots or excess oils but is not the best for eczema.
- **German Chamomile:** With its aromatic and slightly bitter taste, this herb is packed with flavonoids, volatile oils and bitters. It has great anti-inflammatory, anti-allergenic and antispasmodic properties and is a relaxant. Great for eczema, skin inflammation, irritations or rashes, so it is great for eczema and infant cradle cap.
- **Neem Leaf:** You can use this as an oil or ingest it for its anti-inflammatory response or as a powerful antioxidant. Cultivated from the neem plant as oil or used as a tea, this herb works on acne, pimples, and various types of skin rashes, like eczema.

Diet For Skin Issues: Eating lots of fruits, leafy greens and whole grains containing vitamins A, E, C and D. Vitamins will help reduce inflammation, balance hormones and have great antimicrobial properties. Zinc has been known to manage oil production on skin, and drinking lots of water is always key.

4. Anxiety & Depression

- **Valerian:** Valerian is used as a calming sedative to help ease anxiety, nervous tension, stress and depression. It can be taken as drops and can take one to two weeks to fully start kicking in.
- **Lemon Balm:** Belonging to the mint family, this herb produces a calming effect on the body and also helps to improve appetite. It also boosts cognitive function and is commonly ingested in the form of tea.
- **Ashwagandha:** A powerful herb to boost mood, which is great for people who suffer from anxiety, stress and depression. This herb also has anti-inflammatory properties and can help regulate blood sugar levels in the body. You can take it as a powder, tablet and as a tea.

Diet For Anxiety & Depression: Eating a balanced diet with vegetables being the large portion of your meal followed by smaller portions of protein and whole grains. Exercise, 2.5 litres of water daily, a good night's sleep and fresh air can be a powerful road to recovery.

5. Colds & Fevers

- **Garlic Ginger & Lemon:** A popular combination to help induce sweat to reduce temperature and quell high fevers. Normally prepared in tea, you can drink this 3–4 times per day to help manage symptoms.

- **Boneset & Cayenne:** Very useful with respiratory problems during viral flu seasons by stimulating immunity against viral infections. It is also great for congestion in the nasal passage to reduce swelling.
- **Elderberry & Yarrow:** This mixture can also aid in reducing cold and flu symptoms by reducing fever, stimulating appetite and easing coughing due to its anti-inflammatory properties. It can be taken in tea.

Diet For Cold & Flu: First, reduce sugar and dairy in your diet immediately. Stock up on lots of water. Fresh fruits and vegetables in smoothies can make them easier to take. Intermittently fasting can help the body stimulate the immune system and speed up recovery.

6. Menopausal Symptoms

- **White Willow:** An amazing herb that is very good for fevers and joint pains because it contains salicylic acid, similar to aspirin. This herb has anti-inflammatory, analgesic and antirheumatic properties, and it's astringent in its effect, making this herb essential during menopause to protect bones and reduce hot flushes.
- **Chaste Tree:** This amazing herb is a great hormone regulator, sleeping aid and progestogenic. Chaste trees have been used to help ease premenstrual syndrome, period pains and menopausal issues. The berries from the chaste tree help stabilise progesterone and oestrogen in the body and help you relax.
- **Black Cohosh:** A popular herb that acts as a sedative. Its expectorant, oestrogenic and anti-inflammatory properties make this herb very effective in managing hormones. This herb works well for nerves and keeps bones strong. Studies show that hot flashes are reduced by 26% amongst women who use this herb.

Diet For Menopausal Symptoms: First, reduce sugar in your diet immediately. Stock up on lots of water, fresh fruits and leafy greens. Intermittent fasting can help the body stimulate hormonal balance and keep bones strong.

Chapter 5

Fighting Obesity

Obesity is when your body fat content is way too high – beyond what is deemed healthy for the individual – and is usually accompanied by certain types of health complications. The pervasiveness of obesity has increased by 67% in men and 60% in women since 2020. This has a lot to do with COVID-19 restrictions, which means many were working from home and spending less time outside. Furthermore, obesity prevalence exists in low socioeconomic areas in the UK, as mentioned in the John Henryism section. There is clear and measurable data to convey the correlation between people who come from less-affluent areas and disease. This speaks to overworking, stress, easy access to cheap food and poor dietary choices.

The Obesogenic Environment

An obesogenic environment is a present-day term used to describe a plethora of environmental factors that can encourage individuals or communities to become unhealthy in their weight. Those living in an environment where access and availability are constant, and the price of typically unhealthy food is easily affordable, then we can start to see a real challenge in weight management. Since weight gain is often based on an individual's deregulation of food intake, it is safe to say that weight is a direct physiological adaptation to our environment. Besides a very small portion of society with specific types of metabolic disorders, such as hypothyroidism, the overconsumption of food with little to no exercise is the key reason for obesity.

9 Most Common Causes of Obesity

Back in 2003, the World Health Organisation, alongside the Food and Agriculture Organisation, shared their findings on how many chronic diseases have their inception in poor, unhealthy lifestyles. This means little to no exercise and the overconsumption of energy-dense foods (food rich in calories).

- Physical inactivity
- Overeating
- Genetics
- Diets high in simple carbohydrates
- Frequency of eating
- Medications
- Psychological factors
- Diseases such as hypothyroidism, insulin resistance, polycystic ovary syndrome, and Cushing's syndrome are also contributors to obesity.

What Is the Fastest Way to Cure Obesity?

1. **Regular physical activity:** Exercise is paramount to reducing obesity, improving body circulation and elevating serotonin levels. Some key points to consider are that exercising will help burn fat, it will help with energy balance so you are not storing more energy as fat, and it will also help you feel better.
2. **Changing your habits:** Habits are based on our ritualistic behaviour on a day-to-day basis. There are acquired habits that result in obesity, which can make things difficult to create new habits that are more in line with an effective health/ weight loss journey.

3. **Eating a balanced diet:** This is going to be the fundamental and most important part of your transformation. What we put in our bodies is going to either weaken, inflame or slow the body down. There are essential micro and macrominerals that need to be ingested daily in order to experience true health. A balanced diet focuses on half your plate being filled with greens and/or cooked vegetables, while the other half should be split between a protein and complex carb source.

4. **Getting enough sleep:** Epidemiological research shows that lack of proper sleep can have a massive impact on weight gain. This is because ghrelin, the hunger hormone, is deeply impacted by levels of sleep and is elevated if proper sleep is not achieved. Get good quality sleep every night by avoiding late-night snacks and drinking herbal teas, such as camomile teas or valerian root, to help calm down and relax.

5. **Nutritional therapy:** This form of therapy deals with all aspects of your health – stress, food addiction, stress eating, emotional eating, etc. Seeking counselling can be very helpful in exploring your relationship with food, help you structure your nutritional intake, manage your weight and even help you structure how much food you consume.

How To Get Rid of Hypertension

Discovered in 1869 by Italian physician Scipione Riva Rocci by measuring systolic pressure, hypertension is caused by abnormal blood pressure in the arteries. Hypertension is the accumulation of fatty deposits in the arteries, which means the amount of blood flow thins and more pressure is needed to force enough blood to keep flow consistent. One of the many worrying things about hypertension is that it can go unnoticed, and studies show almost one-third of people with high blood pressure or hypertension are completely unaware. The main reason for this is that hypertension has no obvious symptoms to alert you to its presence unless it is severe. There are several effective ways to determine whether or not you have hypertension. You can go for regular check-ups, especially if it runs in your family, or use a home blood pressure kit. Your normal systolic blood pressure should be 120, and diastolic blood pressure should be less than 80.

Signs Of Hypertension

- Severe headaches
- Nosebleeds
- Fatigue or confusion
- Vision problems
- Chest pain
- Difficulty breathing
- Irregular heartbeat
- Blood in the urine

Causes of Hypertension

- **Smoking:** Smoking has an effect on your blood pressure by speeding up your heart rate, and because of the cocktail of chemicals in cigarettes, it narrows blood vessels by causing inflammation. This inflammation constricts blood vessels, especially because of the nicotine content.
- **Being overweight or obese:** Being overweight can place a lot of pressure on the heart, forcing it to work way harder than necessary. The key issue is that all that additional work puts a lot of strain on the arteries and ultimately causes your blood pressure to rise.
- **Lack of physical activity:** Exercise is a great way to keep a healthy heart. People who do not participate in consistent physical activities tend to have higher heart rates, and exercise helps keep the heart in healthy shape by reducing inflammation. Consequently, carrying extra weight affects

mobility and the ability to exercise regularly, which means the heart starts to overwork and ultimately fails over time.

- **Too much salt in the diet:** Often, when we think of too much salt, we do not consider the kidneys or how they relate to hypertension.

   Typically, the kidneys will filter more than 120 quarts (4 cups of water in units) daily, removing toxins and unwanted waste from cells. If you consume too much salt in your diet, it puts a strain on the kidneys, and they will struggle to remove unwanted waste or fluid, which builds up and affects your blood pressure.

- **Stress:** When you are experiencing any form of stress, your body releases a rush of hormones that increase your heart rate. Stress also constricts your blood vessels, affecting your blood pressure. Even though we have no solid scientific proof that stress by itself causes long-term hypertension, it's definitely an accomplice to poor cardiovascular conditions.

How To Reduce Hypertension

- **Eat healthier:** Healthy eating can do amazing things to the human body and sustain life. Healthy eating sits on three basic principles: structure, portion control and nutrition. This means you have to structure your eating patterns and nutritional content by developing a healthy relationship with food. Veggies should always be dominant in your diet, followed by a good amount of protein and complex carbs for fibre. The less junk you eat, the less inflamed and healthier your heart will be.

- **Change oils:** Some of the most popular oils are very problematic to your circulatory and cardiovascular health. The body needs healthy essential fats, such as HDL (high-density lipoprotein), that contribute to our health. Oils like vegetable, sunflower, soy and rapeseed oil are all toxic to the body once heated and will not help the body function correctly. Extra virgin coconut oil, extra virgin hemp, avocado and grapeseed oil are all great cooking oils with high smoke points.

- **Exercise more:** Exercising at least five times a week for at least 30 minutes can help increase heart strength and health. The stronger and healthier your heart is, the more effortlessly your heart pumps blood through your arteries. It takes about 30 days to see exercise impact your blood pressure, so keep consistent. Due to the link to bad cholesterol, exercise helps reduce plaque build-up in the arteries.

- **Lose a bit of weight:** Being overweight can lead to high blood pressure, so dropping weight is essential to normalising your blood pressure levels. Studies show that every 20 pounds of weight loss can potentially reduce systolic pressure anywhere from 5–20 points. Weight loss is a mixture of a caloric deficit (use up more energy than your store) and hormonal balance. By using calorie-restrictive diets, you reduce the amount of insulin in the body, which would otherwise store excess calories as fat. Exercise helps strengthen the body and increases your metabolism.

- **Reduce alcohol consumption:** Drinking alcohol can further constrict blood vessels and worsen hypertension. This happens because of renin, an enzyme released by the kidneys into the bloodstream as a response to depleted sodium levels or when blood pressure falls. In simple terms, alcohol consumption triggers the hormones and enzymes in the kidneys that influence blood pressure. So, try to avoid any alcohol consumption if you have been diagnosed with hypertension.

Conclusion

Hypertension is regularly controlled by medication, which is very important in the day-to-day management of blood pressure levels. Until you are disciplined enough, knowledgeable and have the resources to regulate your blood pressure with the help of a nutritionist, dietician or professional consultant, you should stay on your medication. There are herbs and other natural ways to regulate your blood pressure, but make sure to be safe and take your time. Natural healing takes a lot of time – typically nine months to a year of consistent work to truly have a profound impact that will strengthen the body enough to self-regulate blood pressure.

Reducing Type 2 Diabetes

Type 2 diabetes affects roughly one in ten people over 40 in the UK, and over 90% of the diagnosed cases of diabetes in the UK are type 2. Type 2 diabetes is when you develop insulin resistance, causing excess sugar in the blood. This means your body doesn't respond to insulin efficiently, making it difficult to absorb and utilise sugar from the food you consume. Type 2 diabetes can be kept under control, typically through medication, a balanced diet, physical exercise and hydration. There is a strong link between family history, lineage and type 2 diabetes. However, multiple variable factors also determine your diagnosis, such as race, physical activities and nutritional deficiencies.

Factors That Contribute to Type 2 Diabetes

- **Weight:** Having excess weight can drastically contribute to type 2 diabetes. In fact, studies show it's one of the main causes.
- **Fat distribution:** Fat distribution in the body is a key factor in type 2 diabetes. For example, fat stored in your belly area presents greater risk as opposed to your hips and thighs. You are at high risk if you are male, measuring 40 inches or more around the waist or female and 35 inches or more around the waist.
- **Lack of physical activities:** Physical activities help control weight and promote insulin sensitivity. If you are not active or

exercising, you could put yourself at a great risk of developing type 2 diabetes.

- **Family history:** New research in epigenomics suggests that you can pass on nutritional markers to the next generation. This means you are at a greater risk if others in your family have diabetes.
- **Race and ethnicity:** We are not quite sure why Black people have a higher chance of diabetes compared to Caucasians. One theory is the well-researched link between socioeconomic class and disease. In the West, the percentage of Black to white people is disproportionate, so economic access to healthy food becomes challenging – mixed with other variable factors, such as age, insulin sensitivity and genetics.
- **Blood lipid levels:** Processed foods high in bad fats can increase triglycerides, which can lead to pre-diabetic conditions.
- **Pregnancy-related risks:** Women can develop type 2 diabetes after struggling with gestational diabetes during pregnancy. If the baby is in excess of nine pounds, the mother can be at a greater risk of developing diabetes.

4 Factors That Can Help Reverse Type 2

Diabetes

- **Reduce high-glycaemic carbs:** You have to significantly reduce the amount of starch-based carbs in your diet. Carbs from white pasta, bread, rice, potatoes and sugary products will keep blood sugar elevated and more problematic. Switch to whole grains and vegetables for carbs.
- **Weight loss:** Excess weight can make you more susceptible to type 2 diabetes, and visceral fat can lead to insulin resistance. To drop weight, you need to keep insulin levels under control. You can do this by eating a more balanced diet, keeping

hydrated, exercising often to help burn fat and increasing everyday physical activities.

- **Exercise:** Exercise is key in regulating blood sugar and can make your body more insulin sensitive, which will help your body utilise more energy from stored fat and sugars floating in the bloodstream. You should work out, walk, jog and take classes to keep the body burning fat and will lower your HbA1c value by 0.7 per cent.

- **Nutrition**: The right nutrition can be of great value to help regulate sugar levels, improve HDL (good cholesterol) and reduce LDL (bad cholesterol). Vitamin D3 is a very effective nutrient when it comes to pancreatic diseases, including diabetes. Chromium is also key in helping reverse type 2 diabetes because it's been shown to help sugar in the blood get into cells. This is beneficial because the less sugar floating in the blood, the better the condition will get. Vitamin B1 (thiamine) helps reduce kidney disease in type 2 diabetes, helps convert food to energy and helps the body metabolise fats and proteins. Get as much nutrition as possible from raw veggies and fruits.

Fibroids in Black Women

Fibroids are noncancerous tumours that tend to grow in the uterus and can be as big as a football to the size of a small pea. Two-thirds of the population of women will experience fibroids at some point, and a majority of the time, the women who tend to experience fibroids are over 40 years old. Some women will not experience any noticeable symptoms, while some women will experience significant pain, bleeding, fertility problems and back aches. The troubling reality is that Black women are often three times more likely to have fibroids issues compared to other ethnic groups. Black women statistically have them more frequently, develop more earlier and have more severe symptoms due to larger growths. My assessment of fibroids, like most other diseases that affect the Black population, can be linked back to John Henryism. As mentioned at the beginning of Chapter 4, low-income socioeconomic status is linked to an increase in disease in communities. Other variable factors also play a major role, such as low vitamin D3 levels in Africans and Caribbeans in the diaspora. Up to a quarter of Black women between the ages of 18–30 will have fibroids in comparison to roughly 6% of white women. Furthermore, by age 35, the percentage of Black women who will experience fibroids shoots up to about 50–60%. Stress, epigenomics, lack of physical exercise, poor diet and education, and an increase in oestrogen are all contributing factors. In the UK's Black culture, we seem to be generally less concerned about food-related diseases because food is symbolic and considered a love language. For example, our grandparents, parents and other loved ones look at feeding others as a sign of affection or care. However, with each new generation, we are more aware mentally, emotionally and physically. This means we look after our health a bit more, being more self-aware about what and how much we consume and how it affects us.

Symptoms

Often, women who have fibroids won't overtly experience any symptoms. However, for those who experience symptoms, it can be modulated by the location, size and even the number of fibroids, resulting in a unique experience.

- Heavy menstrual bleeding
- Menstrual periods lasting more than a week
- Pelvic pressure or pain
- Frequent urination
- Difficulty emptying the bladder
- Constipation
- Backache or leg pains

Biological Factors that Contribute to Fibroids

- **Genetic changes:** Some fibroids are hereditary, from epigenetic markers that have been passed down, raising a person's risk. When mixed with a lack of a healthy lifestyle, these genes can easily be activated.
- **Hormones**: High levels of oestrogen mixed with the low presence of progesterone seem to influence the development of fibroids. Typically, chronic stress or even regular high-stress levels convert progesterone into cortisol. This excess availability of oestrogen can make fibroids worse.
- **Other growth factors:** Insulin-like growth factors are proteins that affect the size and number of fibroids in the uterus. This is stimulated by the liver, which also produces these factors in response to hormone imbalance.

Some Tips to Help Reduce Fibroids

- **Limit high-sodium processed and packaged foods:** High sodium affects kidney function, which is linked to high blood pressure, which can cause severe fibroids. Minimise salt intake and use Celtic or organic rock salts, which are less damaging. Avoid processed foods and switch to more home-cooked organic foods that incorporate more fruits and veggies.
- **Increase vitamin D3 levels:** There is extensive research on the connection between low vitamin D3 levels and fibroids, so please get more sunlight. Supplement this by incorporating oily fish, eggs, chestnuts and mushrooms into your diet to help get enough vitamin D3.
- **Intermittent fasting:** Fasting can help regulate hormones that could have otherwise become a factor for fibroid growth. When done correctly and with the right nutritional balance, we can give the body the right type of nutrition, especially antioxidants that promote cellular health.

- **Lose weight, especially around the waist:** Fat cells are known to increase oestrogen levels in the body, and as mentioned before, too much oestrogen can cause fibroid growth. Exercise regularly and maintain a healthy, balanced diet to help reduce weight.
- **Avoid or limit alcohol:** Alcohol is known to promote the overproduction of hormones and can thus stimulate more fibroid growth. Moreover, dehydration caused by alcohol also makes fibroid symptoms worse. An alcohol addiction programme can help if you struggle with this. And as always, keep your body hydrated.
- **Some herbs for fibroids:** There are a plethora of effective herbs that can help shrink fibroids, and they are powerful, especially alongside a healthy lifestyle and diet. Burdock root tea, ginger tea, dandelion root leaf, dong quai and bioflavonoids in green tea can all reduce inflammation in fibroids.

Chapter 6

The Importance of Vitamin D

Vitamin D is a fat-soluble vitamin that stores itself in adipose tissue in the human body. Two key dietary functions of vitamin D in the body include aiding the body to absorb calcium and phosphorus. Vitamin D also helps the body by supporting the immune and central nervous system, regulating insulin, helping lung function and influencing the expression of cancer genes and cardiovascular health. There are two different types of vitamin D: ergocalciferol (Vitamin D2) and cholecalciferol (Vitamin D3). Vitamin D3 is mainly sourced from natural sunlight or dietarily from animal fat, while vitamin D2 is a plant-based vitamin primarily found in mushrooms. Your body uses sunlight's ultraviolet waves to absorb the majority of our vitamin D through the skin, with only about 10% of our vitamin D coming from food sources. The recommended daily amount for vitamin D3 is about 4,000 International Units as the general standard, and you are recommended to be out in the sun for 10–30 minutes with sunscreen. However, people of African and Caribbean descent experience the highest vitamin D deficiencies because of melanin. The presence of melanin reduces the production of vitamin D in the skin. As a result, I recommend that people of African and Caribbean descent in the diaspora get more sun exposure than 30 minutes at a time throughout the day. Use sunscreen to be safe because people of colour can develop melanoma, too. Be very careful if you have a medical condition that leaves you susceptible to intense heat.

How to use Vitamin D3

There are many different types of vitamin D supplements and products floating in the market, and it is very difficult to tell which ones are best to take. What I do recommend is liquid drops or a spray, as they are more bioavailable when in liquid form. This does not mean all liquid forms are great, and I recommend speaking with a professional consultant to guide you on what is best for you. You can take vitamin D by mouth, which is best absorbed when taken after a meal. As far as diet goes, oily fish, seafood and other animal fat products can help you up your vitamin D3 levels. The recommended dose is anywhere from 800–1000 IU; however, if you have a medical condition, are menopausal or experience any acute respiratory illness or fibroids, then 4000 IU daily can reduce inflammation in the body.

What Causes a Vitamin D Deficiency?

Several medical conditions can lead to a vitamin D deficiency in the body and may cause several other health problems.

- **Cystic fibrosis, Crohn's disease and celiac disease:** All of these conditions will prevent the efficient absorption of vitamin D by their effect on the small intestines.
- **Weight loss surgeries**: One of the many side effects of weight loss surgery is the way they deeply affect your intestines and make nutrients difficult to absorb. This can make vitamin D levels in the body drop and should be monitored by a health professional.
- **Obesity:** Low vitamin D levels are often associated with people with a BMI of more than 30 because adipocytes will isolate vitamin D by not releasing it into the bloodstream.

This means larger people need to take more vitamin D to have enough for normal body function.

- **Kidney and liver diseases:** These types of conditions tend to reduce the volume of essential enzymes needed to convert vitamin D into a useful form, which leads to less vitamin D being bioavailable.

What Other Factors Can Cause a Vitamin D Deficiency?

- **Age:** The skin's ability to make vitamin D lessens with age.
- **Mobility:** People who are homebound or are rarely outside (for example, people in nursing homes and other facilities) are not able to use sun exposure as a source of vitamin D.
- **Skin colour:** Melanated people with darker complexion will struggle to get enough vitamin D due to melanin's suppression of vitamin D.

What Medications Can Cause a Vitamin D Deficiency?

Yes, vitamin D levels can be lowered by certain medications. These include:

- **Laxatives**: They hurry food through the gut and, as a result, give the body less time to fully absorb nutrients like vitamins A, D, E and K.
- **Steroids:** Some steroids, like prednisone, can inhibit enzymes responsible for metabolising vitamin D.
- **Cholesterol-lowering drugs**: Cholesterol plays a massive part in vitamin D synthesis, and drugs like statin can reduce cholesterol, thus reducing vitamin D production.
- **Seizure-control drugs:** Anti-seizure drugs, such as phenobarbital, affect the bioactivation of vitamin D metabolism.

Please let your doctor know about any new medication and if the medication they prescribe impacts vitamin D levels in the body. You can get vitamin D supplements to help counter the dropping levels of vitamin D in your body.

Vitamins & Their Function

- **Vitamin A:** Vitamin A is a fat-soluble vitamin made up of several compounds, such as retinoic acid, retinol, retinal and other carotenoids. The key functions of vitamin A are in the immune system, eyesight, skin health and cellular growth. Vitamin A is stored in the liver to be released when needed and is mainly available in oily fish, liver, eggs, leafy greens and yellow or orange fruits. Dry skin, dry eyes, poor wound healing, acne breakouts and even fertility issues can be affected by a vitamin A deficiency. The daily recommended dosage is around 800 mcg and 700 mcg for women over 18.
- **Vitamin B1:** Also known as thiamine, B1 is essential for glucose metabolism and extracting energy from carbohydrates. Thiamine is water-soluble and essential to heart, muscle and nerve health by controlling the flow of electrolytes. Since thiamine is not stored in the body, it means humans need thiamine on a consistent basis. The recommended daily allowance for adult males is about 1.2mg and 1.1mg for females over 18. Food groups rich in thiamine include beans, lentils, fish, fortified cereals, green peas and whole-grain bread.
- **Vitamin B2:** Also known as riboflavin, vitamin B2 is a very important component in modulating the co-enzymes involved in cellular growth and breaking down fats, steroids and medications. It is part of the B complex vitamins, which is a group of B vitamins that play a major role in energy metabolism. You need riboflavin daily. The bacterium in your gut produces a very small amount, so a daily intake of 1.3 mg for men and 1.1 mg for women is essential for daily health.

Foods rich in riboflavin include asparagus, broccoli, grain products, eggs, liver, fish and other fortified cereals.

- **Vitamin B3:** Also known as niacin, vitamin B3 is a water-soluble vitamin that also plays an important role in converting nutrients into usable energy. It also converts fat to cholesterol and repairs our DNA. Some of the major benefits of B3 include better cognitive function, reduced blood pressure, balanced blood-fat levels and improved skin health. Sources of niacin in food include liver, salmon, turkey, chicken breast, wild rice, nutritional yeast, brown rice, squash, cashew/peanuts and chestnut mushrooms. The daily recommended allowance in adults is 16 mg for men and 14 mg for women. You need this daily, as niacin does not stay in the body.

- **Vitamin B5:** Also known as pantothenic acid, vitamin B5 is a water-soluble vitamin that is needed daily and is one of the most important vitamins for human life. Besides breaking down fat and carbohydrates for energy, it also plays a critical role in the production of red blood cells, healthy sexual experience/organs, nervous system improvement, healthy digestive system and the regulation of cortisol production, which is a stress hormone. We need about 5 mg for both men and women on a daily basis. Some rich food sources of vitamin B5 include broccoli, whole grains, nuts, beans, peas, lentils, eggs and poultry.

- **Vitamin B6:** Also known as pyridoxine, vitamin B6 is a water-soluble vitamin that contributes to red blood cell production, helps with the formation of DNA and RNA, and helps reduce any excess amino acids that can interfere with heart health. Vitamin B6 also helps antibodies fight viruses and keep blood sugar normal, in addition to other key functions for health. Your recommended daily allowance is 1.3 mg for both men and women. Some great food sources for vitamin B5 include wheat germ, oats, bananas, poultry, salmon, turkey, red peppers and chives.

- **Vitamin B7:** Also known as biotin, this water-soluble B vitamin was initially discovered as Vitamin H. Your cells do not produce biotin but rather bacteria in your gut, such as Bacteroides and Fusobacterium. Aside from metabolising carbs, proteins and fats, biotin is also responsible for the functioning of mucus membranes and the immune system. In fact, biotin can be found in eggs, salmon and leafy greens. Your body will also use biotin to create the amino acids that get transformed into keratin, which is responsible for healthy nails, hair loss prevention and healthy skin. Adults are recommended 30 mcg daily.

- **Vitamin B9:** Also known as folate or folacin, vitamin B9 is a water-soluble vitamin that has several key functions for human survival. Folate plays a key role in cellular division and DNA repair and aids healthy brain and spine development in early pregnancy. You can source good folate or supplements such as foci acid. Some rich B9 food sources include dark leafy greens, brussels sprouts, broccoli, apples, oranges, grapefruits, avocados, whole grains, seafood and liver. Adults need around 200–400 mcg per day, while pregnant women may require 400–600 mcg on a daily basis.

- **Vitamin B12:** Also known as cobalamin, vitamin B12 is also a water-soluble vitamin that is needed on a daily basis. Some of the main functions of B12 are to aid the production of red cells, help as a co-enzyme to make genetic material, repair DNA and also help metabolise energy from food. Vitamin B12 can be stored in the liver for up to five years but still needs daily replenishment to prevent deficiencies causing a lack of energy and muscle weakness. Adults need around 2 mcg daily. Some rich sources include eggs, salmon, beef, fortified veggies and cereals.

- **Vitamin C:** Also known as ascorbic acid, vitamin C is a powerful antioxidant that carries great anti-inflammatory properties that are used on a daily basis. Vitamin C is water-soluble and helps the body absorb iron to help with energy, wound healing, maintaining healthy tissue, teeth and gums, and so much more. Often, when people have sinus issues due to allergies, vitamin C can relieve congestion thanks to its antihistamine effects. Vitamin C is found in a variety of fruits and veggies, such as oranges, kiwi, grapefruits, lemons, brussels sprouts, peppers and broccoli. Vitamin C is not stored in the body; therefore, full-grown adults should take at least 40 mg per day for optimal health.

- **Vitamin K:** This is a fat-soluble vitamin that has multiple key functions in the body. There are two essential types of vitamin K: phylloquinone and menaquinone. Phylloquinone is plant-based – this is where the majority of your vitamin K should come from. You can source it from dark, leafy greens like kale and spinach. Menaquinone is sourced from meat, cheese, fermented soybeans, etc. Vitamin K helps produce some of the proteins necessary for blood clotting and aids in calcium binding for good bone health. Since your body does not immediately store vitamin K, adults need at least 1 mcg per day.

- **Vitamin E:** Also known as tocopherol, vitamin E plays an important role in our body to help maintain good health. Vitamin E is a well-known, powerful antioxidant that can protect cells against free radicals, boost immune response, help skin by promoting the production of collagen and locking in moisture, and help ease cramp pains during the menstrual cycle. Men need at least 4 mg a day and 3 mg per day for women. You can source vitamin E from dark leafy greens, wheat, peanuts, almonds, pumpkin, bell peppers, fish, sunflower seeds, etc.

Minerals & Their Functions

The importance of minerals can never be understated, and we should always focus on feeding the body essential minerals. Let's look at some essential minerals, what they do, and how they impact the body.

- **Calcium:** Sir Humphry Davy first isolated this compound in 1808 when he was experimenting with lime and mercuric oxide, explaining the name's root meaning in "lime". Calcium is popularly known to strengthen teeth and bones. However, what many may not know is that calcium plays a vital role in nerve signalling, blood clotting, regulating metabolism and muscle relaxation and contractions – it can help relax the muscles caused by cramps as well. If you are deficient in calcium, you may experience muscle cramping, burning sensations in your fingers, facial spasms and bone fragility. The daily recommendation for adults is around 700–1000 mg per day and is best absorbed when you are also consuming good amounts of vitamin D. Calcium can be found in kale, collard greens, bok choy, broccoli, fish, almonds, yoghurts, bone broths, etc.

- **Sodium:** Although sodium is the 6th most abundant element on Earth, and it is also highly reactive. Through the electrolysis of caustic soda in 1807, sodium and its properties were first studied by Sir Humphry Davy. Sodium plays a very important role in human biology, and if you are deficient in sodium, it can lead to serious health issues. Electrolytes that regulate water levels and carry ions may malfunction if the sodium levels are too low. In that case, hyponatraemia can develop, leading to lethargy, confusion and serious fatigue. The main dietary source of sodium is salt, and the daily recommended allowance is no more than 6 g per day. A very good source of salt for cooking is Celtic salt because of its properties, such as its low sodium content, while being packed full of other rich minerals.

- **Potassium:** The 8th most abundant element on Earth, potassium, was first discovered in 1807. Potassium plays a major role in muscle contraction, impulse conduction, brain health and fluid balance. You need around 4,700 mg daily for optimum health as an adult, but consuming this much can be challenging. You'd need about 13–14 bananas a day if that was your only source. A balanced diet packed with fruits like apricots, orange prune, grapefruits and vegetables including spinach, kale, butternut squash and potatoes can add some variety.

- **Magnesium:** Magnesium oxide was also discovered by Sir Humphry Davy during his experiments via electrolysis. There are different types of magnesium that exist, and they all vary in terms of bioavailability, medical use and side effects. Magnesium is a cofactor for over 300 enzymes and, therefore, plays key roles in nerves, muscles, blood pressure, blood sugar regulation and cognitive function. The different types of magnesium include magnesium glycinate, magnesium chloride, magnesium lactate, magnesium malate, magnesium taurate, magnesium sulfate and magnesium oxide. Magnesium citrate is the most common type of magnesium available in supplement form and in everyday foods, as it is the most bioavailable form of magnesium. Typically, the human body has up to 25 grams of magnesium – 50–60% resides in the bones, some in tissue and less than 1% in the blood serum. The daily allowance for adults is 400 mg in men and about 320 mg in women. Some of the best sources of magnesium include spinach, kale, nuts, pumpkin seeds, tuna, brown rice and chicken.

- **Phosphorus**: Brandt Hamburg first isolated this mineral in 1669 through the evaporation of heated urine residue. Eighty-five per cent of phosphorus in the body resides in the bones and teeth, while a small amount resides in the cells and tissue. Key functions of phosphorus include helping the kidneys filter out waste, maintaining healthy teeth and bones, contracting muscles and producing DNA and RNA. A phosphorus deficiency may lead to bone disease and can even stunt growth in children. The best sources of phosphorus are lentils, nuts, dairy products and whole grains. The daily allowance for phosphorus in adults is about 700 mg and 1,250 mg for children aged 9–18.

- **Iodine:** Iodine plays an essential role in thyroid function and helps produce thyroid hormones. It was isolated in 1818 by French scientist Barnard Courtois while experimenting with seaweed ash. Iodine is crucial to brain and bone development in foetuses and during the baby's infant stages. The thyroid is a key factor in metabolism, which plays a big role in cardiovascular function, digestive health and muscle health. The daily recommendation for iodine in adults is about 15 mcg and 120 mcg for children. There are several rich food sources that are high in iodine that reside in everyday foods. Some of these foods include seaweed (Irish Moss), liver, eggs, chicken, oysters and fish.

- **Iron:** Iron is a key mineral that is stored in the human body as ferritin**,** which is found in bone marrow, liver, bones, muscles, etc. Iron is transported in the body to the protein that binds iron in the blood. The human body utilises iron to make haemoglobin, which carries oxygen throughout the body. Iron is also used to make a hormone called hepcidin, which is found in the liver. From a dietary standpoint, there are two types of iron that should be noted: heme iron and non-heme iron. Heme iron is derived from animal protein and is more bioavailable to the body, and heme iron is derived from a plant-based diet. Non-heme iron sources include spinach, kale, nuts, seeds and different types of fruits, all of which require vitamin C to boost uptake. However, heme iron food sources include fish, meat and poultry. Iron's primary function is to help deliver oxygen to muscles and help with energy metabolism. The recommended daily allowance for an adult male is anywhere from 16–18 mg per day and 12 mg per day for adult women.

- **Zinc:** This trace mineral is a very important mineral for the body and is essential to DNA production. First identified in

1746, zinc is widely found in both plant-based and animal-based sources. Oysters have more zinc per serving than any other food available, while spinach, green peas and mushrooms are some of the richest vegetable sources for zinc. As far as fruits go, avocados and blackberries are commonly regarded as the top two fruit sources for zinc. The functions of zinc in the body include maintaining a healthy nervous system, facilitating immune system functions by reducing oxidative stress, healing wounds by enabling the synthesisation of collagen, reducing inflammation, reacting with enzymes and helping with age-related diseases. Zinc is the second most abundant mineral in the body after iron, but since the body cannot produce zinc, it needs 11 mg daily for adult males and 8 mg for adult females.

- **Copper:** It was said that the Sumerians first utilised copper in the ancient kingdoms. However, we know that copper was also used in Ancient Egypt to sterilise wounds and surgical tools and even to purify water, according to the Ebers Smith Papyrus. What we have learned in modern times is that copper helps the uptake of iron in the body, acts as an antioxidant to protect DNA and releases electrically charged ions that help generate energy via melanin. Rich food sources for copper include liver, oysters, spirulina, shiitake mushrooms, leafy greens and dark chocolate. The daily recommended allowance is 1–1.5 mg per day, but please note that zinc can interfere with copper uptake.

Conclusion

The benefits of minerals and vitamins in the body cannot be overstated. These essential nutrients play crucial roles in maintaining overall health and well-being. Minerals such as calcium, iron, magnesium and zinc are vital for the bodily systems to properly function, including bone health, muscle contraction, oxygen transport and immune function. Similarly, vitamins such as A, C, D and B are essential for supporting numerous physiological processes, including vision, immune response, energy production and nerve function.

Minerals and vitamins act as cofactors and catalysts for enzymatic reactions, ensuring that essential processes occur efficiently. They are involved in DNA synthesis, cell division and tissue repair, promoting growth and development. Additionally, these nutrients possess antioxidant properties, helping to neutralise harmful free radicals and protect cells from oxidative damage.

Adequate intake of vitamins and minerals is associated with numerous health benefits. They contribute to a strong immune system, reducing the risk of infections and chronic diseases. They promote healthy skin, hair and nails and support the maintenance of healthy body weight. Furthermore, minerals and vitamins are essential for cognitive function and mental well-being, playing a role in mood regulation and brain health.

While a balanced diet should provide most of the necessary vitamins and minerals, certain individuals may require supplementation due to specific dietary restrictions, health conditions or life stages. However, it is important to note that excessive intake of certain vitamins and minerals can have adverse effects on health. Therefore, it is crucial to consult with a healthcare professional to determine individual needs and ensure appropriate supplementation, if necessary.

In summary, minerals and vitamins are indispensable for the optimal health and functioning of the human body. Their diverse roles in various physiological processes make them essential components of a well-rounded and nutritious diet. By understanding and meeting our body's requirements for these nutrients, we can support our overall well-being and enjoy the benefits of a healthy and vibrant life.

A Nutritional Path Back to Eden

Eden is described in the Bible as a place of perfection and bliss. We often look at health as a time-consuming, challenging, unrealistic and sustainable practice that requires some form of perfection. That couldn't be further from the case, and in reality, the concept of Eden in this book refers to the idea of balance, homeostasis, balance and zen as the only true path to health. We often overlook that the civilisation we've built has not sufficiently prioritised connecting quality of life with a healthy mind and soul. What we have done has placed more value on class, economics and ability to influence. This is very troubling given the fact that in the West, we are riddled with processed, high-glycaemic foods with trans-fat and no nutritional value. As mentioned in Chapter 4, there is a massive connection between low economic status and food choices. This suggests that the majority of these people will end up with some form of health complication purely based on the fact that they were born into a class that can barely afford to prioritise healthy eating. We must provide accessibility, education, support and more incentives to live more balanced lives, and we will start to see an increase in generational health. The most important message in this book is to educate yourself on the dangers of poor diet, lack of exercise and constant stress. Once you have been truly enlightened about how poor eating affects future generations via biological markers, only then will you recognise the true reward of health is more life. To start your journey back to Eden, I suggest you start to look at your habits, values, and beliefs regarding food. Consequently, prioritise a balanced lifestyle that allows you to work, rest, eat well, exercise and do things you love without being stuck in survival mode.

"May yo ta t e s e ne r of he h, ba c & f e m"

JoDash

References

Chapter 1

http://www.foodsystemprimer.org/food-production/history-of-agriculture/

https://www.newscientist.com/article/2149848-coldclimate-may-have-driven-ancient-humans-m ove-out-of-africa/ https://soyummy.com/medieval-times-food/

https://www.theelephant.info/culture/2018/02/08/foo d-and-migration-a-culinary-journey-through-e ast-africa/

https://raisingselfawareness.com/african-spiritualityguide/

Carpenter K. J. (2003). A short history of nutritional science: Part 1 (1785-1885). *The Journal of nutrition, 133*(3), 638–645.

https://doi.org/10.1093/jn/133.3.638

Ordish, George, Crawford, Gary W., Nair, Kusum, Fussell, George Edwin, Rasmussen, Wayne D., Mellanby, Kenneth and Gray, Alic William. "Origins of agriculture". *Encyclopedia Britannica*, 4 Feb. 2020, https://www.britannica.com/topic/agriculture. Accessed 12 September 2021.

History Of Food & Agriculture

Chapter 2

Currenti, W., Buscemi, S., Cincione, R. I., Cernigliaro, A., Godos, J., Grosso, G., & Galvano, F. (2021). Time-restricted feeding and metabolic outcomes in a cohort of Italian adults. *Nutrients*, *13*(5), 1651. https://doi.org/10.3390/nu13051651

Hallak MH, Nomani MZ: Body weight loss and changes in blood lipid levels in normal men on hypocaloric diets during Ramadan fasting. Am J Clin Nutr. 1988, 48: 1197–1210.

Noyes, F. R., & Barber-Westin, S. D. (2016, March 18). *Diagnosis and treatment of complex regional pain syndrome.* Noyes' knee disorders: Surgery, rehabilitation, clinical outcomes (Second Edition). https://www.sciencedirect.com/science/articl e/abs/pii/ B9780323329033000408

Rathod, Y. D., & Di Fulvio, M. (2021). The feeding microstructure of male and female mice. *PloS one*, *16*(2), e0246569. https://doi. org/10.1371/journal.pone.0246569

Roky R, Chapotot F, Hakkou F, Benchekroun MT, Buguet A: Sleep during Ramadan intermittent fasting. J Sleep Res. 2001, 10: 319–327. 10.1046/j.1365-2869.2001.00269.x.

Suslov, A. V., Chairkina, E., Shepetovskaya, M. D., Suslova, I. S., Khotina, V. A., Kirichenko, T. V., & Postnov, A. Y. (2021). The neuroimmune role of intestinal microbiota in the pathogenesis of cardiovascular disease. *Journal of clinical medicine*, *10*(9), 1995. https://doi.org/10.3390/jcm10091995

Chapter 3

Aronson, D., 1996. Overview of systems thinking.

Available at /http:// www.thinking.net/Systems_Thinking/systems _ thinking.htmlS. Berkes, F., 2002.

Boehlji, M.D., Hofing, S.L., Schroeder, R.C., 1999. Value chains in the agricultural industries. Department of Agricultural Economics Staff Papers. Purdue University. Bryceson, D., 2000.

Cross-scale institutional linkages: Perspectives from the bottom up. In: Ostrom, E., Dietz, T., Dolsak, N., Stern, P.C., Stonich, S., Weber, E.U. (Eds.), The Drama of the Commons.

National Academy Press, Washington, DC. Berkes, F., Folke, C., 1998. Linking social and ecological systems for resilience and sustainability. In: Berkes, F., Folke, C. (Eds.), Linking Social and Ecological Systems. Cambridge University Press, Cambridge, UK.

Rural Africa at the crossroads: Livelihood practices and policies. ODI Natural Resource Perspectives, vol. 52. London, UK. Cannon, T., 2002. Food security, food systems and liv

Chapter 4

Chaves, J. R., de Souza, C. R. T., Modesto, A. A. C., Moreira, F. C., Teixeira, E. B., Sarraf, J. S., Allen, T. S. R., Araújo, T. M. T., & Khayat, A. S. (2020). Effects of alkaline water intake on gastritis and miRNA expression (miR-7, miR-155, miR-135b and miR-29c). *American journal of translational research*, *12*(7), 4043–4050. Pollack, G. H. (2013). *The fourth phase of water: Beyond solid, liquid, and vapor.* Ebner & Sons.

Cohen, S., & Popp, F. A. (1997). Biophoton emission of the human body. *Journal of photochemistry and photobiology. B, Biology*, *40*(2), 187–189. https://doi.org/10.1016/s1011-1344(97)0005 0-x

Kobayashi M, Kikuchi D, Okamura H (2009) Imaging of ultraweak spontaneous photon emission from human body displaying diurnal rhythm. PLoS ONE 4(7): e6256.

Garjajev. (2009). Crisis in life science.

Garjajev, Friedman, & Leonava-Gariaeva. (2001) Principles of linguistic wave genetics.

Bischof, M. (1995). Biophotons — The light in our cells. Frankfurt: Zweitausendeins.

Popp, A., & Zhang, J. (2000). Mechanism of interaction between electromagnetic fields and living organisms. Science in China, 43 (5), 507–18.

Chapter 5

Grass, F., Klima, H., & Kasper, S. (2004). Biophotons, microtubules and CNS, is our brain a "holographic computer"? Medical Hypotheses, 62, 169–172.

Mayburov, S. N. (2011). Photonic communications and information encoding in biological systems. Quant. Com. Com., 11, 73.

Osteoporosis, Volume 1; Robert Marcus; 2008 Searchinger, T., Heimlich, R., Houghton, R. A., Dong, F., Elobeid, A., Fabiosa, J., Tokgoz, S., Hayes, D., Yu, T. -H. Science, February 7, 2008 (10.1126/science.1151861)

Sun Y., W. C. (2010). Biophotons as neural communication signals demonstrated by in situ biophoton autography. Photochem. Photobiol. Sci.

Chapter 6

Gillespie S, Mason J, Martorell R. How nutrition improves. Geneva: ACC/SCN; 1996. (Nutrition Policy Discussion Paper No. 15

Jennings J, et al., editors. Managing successful nutrition programmes. Geneva: ACC/SCN; 1991. (State-of-the-Art Series, Nutrition Policy Discussion Paper No. 8)

Mason JB, et al. Community health and nutrition programs. *Disease control priorities in developing countries*. 2nd edition. Jamison DT, et al., editors. Washington DC: World Bank; 2006. pp. 1063–1074.

World Bank; UNICEF. Combating malnutrition: Time to act. Gillespie S, McLachlan M, Shrimpton R, editors. Washington DC: World Bank; 2003.

Reading Rainbow Tip: It's important to give your opinion! Would you recommend this book to someone else?

Printed in the United States
by Baker & Taylor Publisher Services